THE GUIDE FOR GUYS

AN EXTREMELY USEFUL MANUAL FOR OLD BOYS AND YOUNG MEN

Library of Congress Cataloging-in-Publication Data Available

1 2 3 4 5 6 7 8 9 10

Published in 2008 by Sterling Publishing Co., Inc.
387 Park Avenue South, New York, NY 10016

Copyright © 2007 Gusto Company under license to JW Cappelens
forlag

Executive editor and original concept by James Tavendale
Designed by Allen Boe
llustrations by www.retroclipart.com, Art Direction Book Co.,Inc.,
www.clipart.com

Distributed in Canada by Sterling Publishing
c/o Canadian Manda Group, 165 Dufferin Street
Toronto, Ontario, Canada M6K 3h6

For information about custom editions, special sales, premium and
corporate purchases, please contact Sterling Special Sales Department at 800-805-5489 or specialsales@sterlingpub.com

Manufactured in China

Sterling ISBN: 978-1-4027-6315-1

THE GUIDE FOR GUYS

AN EXTREMELY USEFUL MANUAL FOR OLD BOYS AND YOUNG MEN

MICHAEL POWELL

STERLING

New York / London
www.sterlingpublishing.com

★

CONTENTS

INTRODUCTION

Gone are the days when a guy could get by on a firm handshake, good aim, and a high tolerance for whiskey. Today you have to be able to make clever small talk, throw a curveball, or even garnish a cocktail with a sprig of mint. In an age when men are practicing yoga and getting manicures, but are still expected to open jars and change flat tires, it's no wonder you may feel like you've lost your bearings.

When attacked in the wild, should you play dead, fight back, or run? What is the proper etiquette when hosting a barbecue? Is there an elegant way to carve a pumpkin? A surefire way to impress your boss? From changing directions gracefully on the dance floor to wielding a circular saw, for burly "guys' guys" to borderline metrosexuals and everything in between, *The Guide for Guys* will make you cultured, efficient, and polite. But never fear, while you're learning to order sushi, avoid jet lag, and write thank you notes, you'll still spend the bulk of your time beefing up on such traditional "manly" skills as swinging a hammer and building a shelter in the wild.

So come on fellas— it's time to tie your own ties, ask for a raise, get the best table in the restaurant, shave without nicking yourself, and train your dog better than your last girlfriend trained you.

READY
SET
GO!

HOW TO USE A COMPASS

A compass is a simple yet very powerful piece of equipment that everyone should learn how to operate. Whether you are up a mountain, or in the middle of the ocean, if you use your compass correctly it will never let you down.

COMPASS ANATOMY

Inside every compass is a red and black arrow called the compass needle. The red part of the needle always points to magnetic north (the earth's magnetic north pole). The turntable around the compass is called the compass housing. The edge of the housing is numbered from 0 to 360 as well as N, E, S, and W (North, East, South, and West).

FIND YOUR BEARINGS

While you are traveling, pay attention to your surroundings and make a mental note of important features and their direction relative to you. For example if there is a line of trees, make a note of the direction in which they are pointing and use these visual clues to help you navigate.

STANDARD COMPASS If you are using a standard compass (like the one provided in this book) and you want to head north, just walk in the direction that the red arrow is pointing; otherwise, you first need to set up your compass to find your bearings. Turn the compass so that the red arrow lines up with the "N" for north, then find your direction on the compass face and start walking.

ORIENTEERING COMPASS The more adventurous, or those interested in the sport of orienteering, will want to try an orienteering compass which includes a see-through base plate, orienting lines and direction of travel arrow. Say you want to travel Northeast. Turn the dial so that the direction of travel arrow is lined up halfway between North and East. Next, keeping the compass flat and making sure that the compass housing doesn't move, turn your body until the red arrow points to N on the compass housing. Now the direction of travel arrow will be pointing Northeast. Pick out a feature in the distance to which the direction of travel arrow is pointing, and start walking towards it. You are now walking in a Northeast direction. Stop and check your bearings every few hundred yards to stay on course.

USING A COMPASS AND MAP

With a little practice, it is easy to navigate in unfamiliar territory using a map and an orienteering compass together.

Suppose you are at A and you want to get to B. Line up points A and B along the edge of the compass, making sure that the direction of travel arrow is pointing away from A. Keeping the compass fixed in this position on the map, carefully twist the compass housing until the orienting lines on the compass housing line up with the vertical meridian lines on the map. The meridian lines run north-south, and on most maps north is at the top.

Now remove the compass from the map and hold it flat in your hand so that the needle can move freely. Turn your body until the red arrow (which will be pointing north) lines up with N on the compass housing. The direction of travel arrow will now be pointing in the correct direction. Fix your eye on a distinctive feature to which the direction of travel arrow is pointing and walk towards it.

If you are lost and you don't have a compass, see page 68, which explains how nature can guide you home.

BALLROOM DANCING FOR GUYS

It is fun, sophisticated, sexy, and it keeps you fit, so it is no surprise that ballroom dancing is making such a sparkling comeback. Dance aficionados generally attribute the end of social partner dancing to the early 1960s, when the Twist appeared. This was the first major rock-and-roll dance in which men and women didn't have to touch each other! Shame. Fortunately, ballroom dancing is timeless, and women still love to be romanced by an elegant guy. Before you put on your dancing shoes, however, here are ten tips to help you to exude smooth confidence:

1. Looking the part actually helps you to adopt the correct posture and poise, so ditch those jeans and slip into something more sophisticated, even if it is just a form-fitting black shirt and pants.

2. Develop good footwork and good style will follow. Make your steps definite (don't drag your feet), and carry more of your weight on the ball of your foot than your heel.

"Either dance well or leave the ballroom."

—*Greek proverb*

WISE MEN SAY

3. Your steps should start from your hip, so that each leg can swing freely from the joint.

4. In general, the faster the song, the shorter the steps.

5. When changing direction, it is easier to maintain your balance when your feet are close together.

6. Make sure you know the direction of movement on the dance floor—usually counterclockwise.

7. If you don't want to stand out from the crowd, dance in the center of the dance floor; this also means you'll be able to move more slowly.

8. Signal to your partner that you are about to start moving by leaning into the step: the greater the lean, the bigger the step. This gives her plenty of warning and prevents you from "popping the clutch," giving her a shaky start.

9. If your partner taps you on the back she is warning you that you are about to collide with another couple.

10. No matter what happens, have fun!

HOW TO DANCE THE WALTZ

The Waltz is a good dance for a beginner. The music is in ¾ time, which means that there are three equal beats to the measure, with the emphasis on the first beat: ONE-two-three, ONE-two-three, etc.

THE CLOSED POSITION To hold your partner correctly, place your right hand under her left arm, and extend your left arm to grasp her right hand. She places her left hand on your shoulder. This is known as the closed position. In this dance the man leads and the woman follows.

LEADING YOUR PARTNER There are four general directions to lead:

1. Forward: guide her toward you by applying pressure with your right hand and gently pulling in your left hand

2. Backward: push her gently away from you and extend your left hand outward

3. Left: push gently with your extended left hand

4. Right: gently pull your right hand to the right

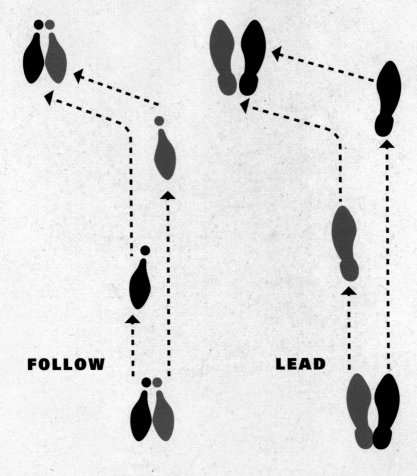

FOLLOW   LEAD

THE BOX STEP There are several Waltz patterns, but the basic pattern is called the Box step, so named because the steps trace a square shape. On the first beat, take one step forward with your left foot. On the second beat, in a single sweeping motion gracefully slide your right foot forward and to the right.

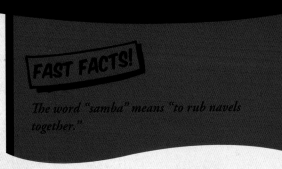
On the third beat, slide your left foot next to your right. On the next three beats, repeat the same movements in reverse: step backward with your right foot; step back and to the left with your left foot; bring your right foot next to your left foot. You should now be back where you started.

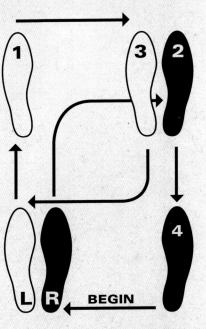

MAJOR BALLROOM DANCE STYLES
CHA-CHA Originally called the Mambo-Rumba, this dance was created by a Cuban violinist named Enrique Jorrín in 1954; it is similar to the Rumba but with a more complicated rhythm danced over two measures of ⁴⁄₄ time.

FOXTROT Invented by American vaudeville actor Harry Fox in New York in 1914, the Foxtrot was made famous by Vernon and Irene Castle. According to legend, Fox couldn't find female dancers who could dance the Two-step, so he added two trots to create the now famous "slow-slow-quick-quick-slow" Foxtrot rhythm.

PASO DOBLE This Latin American dance, based on the Spanish bull-fight, actually originated in southern France. Its name means "two step" in Spanish. It is very dramatic, with sharp movements. The man represents the matador and the woman his cape.

QUICKSTEP Dynamic and fast-paced, this dance is in 2/4 or 4/4 time, like a fast Foxtrot. It evolved in the 1920s from a combination of the Foxtrot, the Charleston, the Shag, the Peabody, and the One-step.

RUMBA One of the most erotic and sensual of the Latin dances, the Rumba has a relatively slow rhythm and lots of hip action and spot turns. It arose in Havana, Cuba, in the 1890s.

SAMBA A vibrant Brazilian dance (think Rio Carnival) with African origins, the Samba is in 2/4 time, but dancers take three steps to every two beats, so it feels like a dance in 3/4 time.

TANGO This dramatic Argentinean dance with a 4/4 measure uses lots of clipped and staccato movements and characteristic "head snaps."

WALTZ The ever-popular Waltz has Austrian peasant origins but first became fashionable in Vienna around the 1780s. It is in 3/4 time with much rotation.

TOOLS AND HOW TO USE THEM

Whither the handyman? There was a time when men knew how to make themselves useful around the house and could fix just about anything. Today, in many cases, the relationship between a man and his tools has grown strained, and tools are being used inefficiently, unsafely, and sometimes just plain incorrectly. Isn't it time you and your tools kissed and made up?

HAMMER Choose the right hammer for the job. Use a claw hammer to pound in and remove nails; a ball-peen hammer, with a round metallic head, to drive a chisel; and a mallet for jobs that require a soft head, such as securing wooden joints or tapping paving slabs into place. A sledgehammer, which has a long handle and a large, flat head, is used to distribute force over a wide area, such as when breaking through masonry or driving fence posts into the ground.

FAST FACTS!

The oldest known tools were discovered by archaeologists at Gona, Ethiopia, during the early 1990s. These stone artifacts were made some 2.5 million years ago.

Always hammer on a solid surface. Grip the hammer firmly at the end of the handle for maximum leverage. Hit the surface squarely using your arm and elbow, rather than merely bending at the wrist. Hit only with the head, not the side. Keep your wrist straight and let the weight of the hammer do most of the work.

Hold a sledgehammer with two hands and use a swinging action that involves the whole torso.

CIRCULAR SAW Make sure that the blade is sharp, otherwise it will overheat during use. Check that the blade is properly seated before you switch it on. Don't expose too much of the blade, or you risk a kickback. The optimum depth of the blade is no more than a quarter inch greater than the thickness of the wood. Avoid cutting into knots, and secure the wood on both sides. Start the saw before making contact with the wood, and wait for the blade to stop fully before removing it.

LADDER Rest the top and bottom of the ladder against a secure and level surface, then test the angle of incline for stability. Face the ladder and place your toes against the ladder base; without bending forward you should be able to reach out and grip a rung at shoulder level with your arms parallel to the floor.

When climbing and descending, keep your hands on the outside of the ladder at all times, and let it slip through your hands, rather than grabbing the rungs. This ensures that you will always have three points of contact with the ladder.

DRILL Wear eye protection every time you drill. Apply gentle pressure, otherwise the drill bit will overheat or the motor will burn out. Withdraw periodically with the drill still running to remove dust from the hole.

Always use the right bit and drill speed for the job:

- Concrete and masonry: use a slow speed, hammer action, and a masonry drill bit with a tungsten carbide tip

- Wood: use a wooden bit at a high speed

- Metal or plastic: use a high-speed steel (HSS) twist drill bit at a slow speed

- Ceramic tiles: use a tile bit at a slow speed

Mark a line on the drill bit with a marker or masking tape, so that you can drill to a predetermined depth. Make sure that the drill is always perpendicular to the drilling surface. When drilling deep or large holes, make a small pilot hole first.

MAINTENANCE

Store tools in a dry, secure place and do not expose them to extremes of temperature. Ensure that tools are kept clean and sharp and that metal tools are oiled regularly to protect them from rust. To remove rust, use steel wool or soak tools in white vinegar. Sand lightly and apply linseed oil to wooden handles once a year.

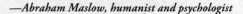

"When the only tool you own is a hammer, every problem begins to resemble a nail."

—*Abraham Maslow, humanist and psychologist*

WISE MEN SAY

MIX THE PERFECT COCKTAIL

Drinks similar to cocktails have been around for a few hundred years, but it was Prohibition in 1920s America that really heralded the age of the cocktail. Bootleg alcohol often tasted unpleasant, so bartenders started mixing it with fruit juices and other ingredients to make it go down easier. Today, making and drinking cocktails is just for fun (and it's legal, unless you decide to distill your own liquor).

COCKTAIL COMPONENTS

Cocktails usually consist of three main components. The first is the base; this is often a spirit, such as gin, vodka, whiskey, or tequila. The second is the mixer, which complements the base and brings out its flavor; common examples include vermouth, fruit juices, wine, soda, cream, eggs, and ice cream. Finally, a third ingredient is sometimes added to provide additional subtlety and possibly color to the drink.

STOCKING YOUR BAR

The main piece of equipment to have on hand is a cocktail shaker. Shakers come in two basic types: European, which has a built-in strainer in the lid, and American, which consists of two flat-bottomed cones that are held together; a separate strainer is then used.

Small metal or glass measures called jiggers are used to determine the correct proportions of the various ingredients. A standard jigger holds about 30 ml (about 1 fl. oz.) of liquid.

Apart from glasses (made out of glass, please, not plastic, which can taint the taste of the cocktail), you'll need lots of ice (cubes and crushed), knives, a chopping board, bowls, swizzle sticks, and—controversial among cocktail purists—an electric blender.

SHAKEN, NOT STIRRED

There are four basic ways to mix a cocktail.

1. SHAKING Fill your cocktail shaker three-quarters full with ice cubes (avoid crushed ice, as it makes the drink watery). Pour the ingredients into the shaker in order of alcohol content, starting with the highest. Hold the shaker in both hands, one at the top and the other at the base, and shake vigorously. When a fine frosty mist forms on the outside of the metal shaker, the drink is ready to be poured into a glass.

2. STIRRING Fill your cocktail shaker and stir the contents with a metal or glass rod. When frost forms on the outside of the shaker, strain the mixture into a glass. A stirred cocktail is less cloudy than one that has been shaken. Drinks with carbonated mixers should not be shaken or stirred; they are "built" directly in the serving glass: add ice cubes, alcohol, then top off with mixer.

3. BLENDING Using an electric blender is a quick and easy way to combine ingredients that do not easily mix, such as cream and bananas. Blend fruit to a smooth consistency before adding ice.

"One martini is all right, two are too many, and three are not enough."

—*James Thurber, author and humorist*

"Do not allow children to mix drinks. It is unseemly, and they use too much vermouth."

—*Steve Allen, comedian and talk-show host*

4. LAYERING Also known as floating, layering a drink involves carefully pouring each ingredient into a glass over the back of a cold spoon, so that they do not mix with each other but instead form separate layers.

THE GARNISH

You can use anything that's colorful or has an interesting shape to decorate your cocktail, but keep it simple and classy. Don't swamp your elegant creation with a bunch of gaudy straws and swizzle sticks. The garnish (fresh fruit, mint sprigs, etc.) should be visually appealing but also refer to the flavors in the cocktail. For example, a slice of lemon indicates that the drink is sharp, while a strawberry or Maraschino cherry suggests something sweet. Some garnishes are standard, such as the olive in a dry Martini.

You can also frost the rim of the glass with either salt (such as for a Margarita) or sugar. The easiest way to do this is to set up two small plates, one with salt or sugar and the other with several slices of lemon. First, twirl the rim of the glass on the fruit, then dip the rim into the salt or sugar.

THE PERFECT MARGARITA

Pour 1½ ounces of tequila, ½ ounce of triple-sec (a strong, sweet, colorless orange-flavored liqueur; Curaçao, Grand Marnier, or Cointreau works well) and 1 ounce of lime juice into a shaker that is three-quarters full of ice cubes. Shake well, then strain into a glass with a salt-frosted rim.

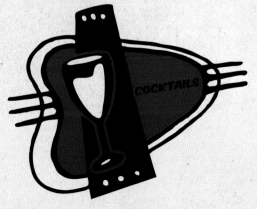

HOLD A BABY

Ah, babies, those precious little bundles of joy. Unfortunately, many guys, if they don't have kids of their own, are afraid to pick them up for fear of breaking them. But there's no need to be intimidated by the little darlings. Sure, they need to be handled with care, but they're tougher than you think. These sure-fire cuddling techniques will ensure that the next time one of your colleagues brings her baby to work, you can boost your sex appeal in the office by appearing to be a natural in the baby-holding department.

CRADLE HOLD

This is the most common way to hold a baby. The baby's head goes in the crook of your arm, which is held flat against your chest, supported by your other arm. Keep the baby's head slightly higher than the body.

In this position you can make lots of eye contact and really interact. If the baby is feeling inquisitive, let her play with your face (noses are a favorite) or grip one of your fingers. Don't put your finger in the baby's mouth. Many babies can also sleep well in this position.

SHOULDER HOLD

Lean the baby across your chest with your hand under its bottom, and use your other hand to support the head. The baby will be comforted by the sound of your heartbeat as she snuggles into your upper chest, or she can look over your shoulder if she's feeling inquisitive. Watch out if she's just been fed, as this is a great position to release trapped wind, which could make the baby vomit over your back.

"A baby is God's opinion that the world should go on."

—*Carl Sandburg, poet, author, and folklorist*

WISE MEN SAY

BELLY HOLD

If the baby is gassy, lay her chest-down over one of your forearms, with the side of her head supported in your hand and her arms and legs straddling your arm. Use your other hand to prevent her from falling, or to gently rub her back.

CHEST HOLD

Place the baby's back against your chest and support him with one arm under his bottom and the other arm over his chest to keep him secure. You can't see the baby's face, but he can take a good look around.

HIP HOLD

When a baby is old enough to support her own head, sit her facing outward, with her bottom on one of your hip bones, and wrap your arm around her waist.

SITTING DOWN

When your arms get tired, sit down with your knees propped up. Lay the baby face-up with head and body resting on your knees and feet at your tummy. This position allows you plenty of interaction.

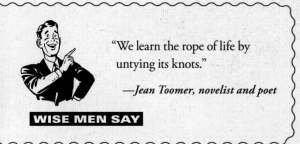

FIVE KNOTS WORTH KNOWING

OVERHAND KNOT

This is the simplest knot and is very secure. It should be used only to tie something permanently, as it is difficult to unknot.

➤ Simply create a loop and push the end of rope through it.

SQUARE KNOT

Known as the reef knot in the UK and as the Knot of Hercules by the ancient Greeks, this is one of the most popular knots. It is used for securing the ends of a rope around something, such as the neck of a sack or a parcel. It can also be used to bind two ropes together, but in situ-

> "We learn the rope of life by untying its knots."
>
> —*Jean Toomer, novelist and poet*

WISE MEN SAY

ations in which safety is an issue opt instead for the more secure fisherman's knot.

•• Hold an end of rope in each hand; tie a left-handed overhand knot followed by a right-handed overhand knot.

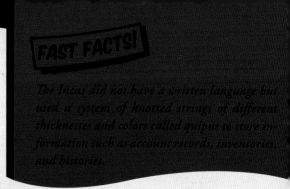

FISHERMAN'S KNOT

This knot is used to tie two ropes of equal thickness together. It is used by fishermen to join fishing line and is very effective with small-diameter string and twine.

•• Tie an overhand knot in one end of the first rope, around the second rope. Then tie an overhand knot in the second rope, around the first rope. Make sure the overhand knots fit snugly against each other when the standing ends are pulled tight.

DOUBLE FIGURE EIGHT

This knot is essential in mountain climbing and in situations in which a rope needs to support a lot of weight without becoming untied.

- ➥ Double up the rope and make a figure-eight shape then feed one end of the rope through the opposite loop. Pull tight. The loop can then be attached to a carabiner.

CLOVE HITCH

The clove hitch is the knot a cowboy would use to tie his horse to a post. This is a widely used knot that puts little strain on the rope fibers because it passes around an object (such as a fence post) in only one direction. It also has the advantage of being quick to tie.

- ➥ Loop the rope once around the post, then bring the end up the other side and pass it underneath the loop at the top. Pull tight.

TRAIN YOUR DOG

Training your dog is actually about learning how to communicate with the animal and understanding the dog's innate behavior and perception of the world. It is not simply a question of making the pooch obey your commands. The main aim of training should be to make your dog happy and confident, because an untrained dog will be unhappy and confused.

HOW TO BE THE LEADER OF THE PACK

Dogs are pack animals, and each pack is governed by a strict hierarchy. In order for your dog to be happy and well adjusted, you must be the top dog, and the dog must be the lowest member of the hierarchy in your family. This then frees the dog from the stress of having to be in charge (for example, a dog that feels he is the pack leader will often fret when you leave the house because he wants to keep you safe).

- Never hit your dog—it only teaches him to be frightened of you and reduces his confidence (only frightened dogs bite and attack; confident dogs are happy and safe). If you show calm authority at all times, he will get the message without your having to resort to violence.

- Project a calm confidence, and express this in your body language; give your dog plenty of attention but only on your terms. For example, if he won't stop barking when you come through the door, ignore him until he stops, then give lots of praise. He'll soon learn to quiet down. Keep your dog below you at all times—don't let him jump up to greet you or jump up on the furniture.

- Before feeding your dog, pretend to eat from his bowl. Dominant dogs always eat first. Don't feed him scraps from the table. Giving away your food sends the unwelcome signal that your dog is dominant. If your dog steals food, however, don't try to get it back, unless it is dangerous (e.g., cooked chicken bones).

LEARN TO UNDERSTAND DOG LANGUAGE

Aside from barking, dogs make a wide range of sounds to communicate their feelings, including:

WHINE This is to attract attention.

WHIMPER This is a sign of serious distress, abject fear or pain, or a very intense pleading signal.

YELP This means "Ouch!" If you step on your dog's tail by accident you'll hear a yelp. Dogs also use this noise to signal to other dogs when play has become too rough, so if your dog accidentally hurts you, be sure to yelp so he gets the message.

GROWL This is a warning sound but is also used in play and play-fighting. A deep and prolonged growl means "Back off!"

SNARL When a dog shows his teeth and snarls he feels threatened, and you definitely need to back off.

HOWL Sometimes this is a sign of distress, but dogs also howl to communicate with other dogs over long distances.

REWARDS AND CORRECTION

Reward good behavior (with enthusiastic praise and small food treats) and correct or ignore bad behavior, but you must do both immediately (within a second) after the behavior has occurred. There is no point in telling the dog off for peeing on the floor or chewing the furniture while you were out, because he won't understand why he is being punished.

CONSISTENCY

Be consistent with what your dog is allowed to do. For example, either he is allowed on the sofa or not; you can't shout at him at times and at other times relent. Make a rule and stick to it. Likewise, use the same gestures and words when giving commands such as "Sit," "Heel," or "Stay."

MIX VOCAL COMMANDS WITH HAND SIGNALS

The quality of your voice is very important. Praise your dog with a high-pitched voice and use a deep voice to correct him when he has done something wrong.

These are the basic commands that every well-trained dog should know:

SIT Stand in front of the dog and hold your hand in front of his nose, as if you were holding a treat; snap your wrist upward as you give the vocal command. Reward him as soon as he puts his bottom on the floor. At first you may have to help him by gently pushing on his bottom.

STAY As you give the command, extend your arm forward with your outstretched palm facing the dog.

HEEL When you first begin training your dog to understand this command, say "Heel" and slap your thigh when he is already walking by your side, then give him lots of praise. Eventually, you can progress to using the command when he is farther away from you.

> "A dog is not considered a good dog because he is a good barker. A man is not considered a good man because he is a good talker."
>
> —*Chuang-tzu, philosopher, 4th century BCE*

WISE MEN SAY

MAKE SMALL TALK

Making small talk isn't just a valuable skill; it's a necessity in most social situations and one that you ignore at your peril. A study at the Stanford University School of Business that tracked MBAs for ten years after they graduated discovered that grade-point averages had little impact on the graduates' success, but their ability to connect with other people did.

If you hate small talk and would prefer your conversations to be peppered with awkward silences, then you are clearly coming at social interaction from the wrong angle. The key to smooth small talk is to make the other person feel comfortable. Who cares if you happen to think it's trivial and artificial? If you at least make the effort, there's less chance that you'll leave a bad impression, and the more you practice, the more natural it will become. Only unskilled talkers find small talk uncomfortable and unnecessary. Recognize that small talk is as important a social skill as good table manners, and try to improve. Here are some ways to keep the conversation flowing:

BE OPTIMISTIC

It is much easier to talk with someone who is being upbeat, rather than complaining. When we can't think of what to say, it's tempting to say something negative, because often it seems easier than making a positive comment; chances are it will make the other person feel awkward.

SPEAK WITH CONFIDENCE

This will make others relax with you and talk more easily. Many people almost consciously do the exact opposite of this and appear nervous, almost as if they want to signal to the other person that they feel just as awkward as they do, and are therefore not a threat. This tactic is misguided, however, and just makes you look like a loser.

MAINTAIN AN OPEN BODY POSTURE

Face the person with whom you are talking, rather than turning sideways and talking to the side of their head; this is another defense mechanism that should be avoided. Don't fold your arms and don't fidget (this includes jangling your keys or the change in your pants pocket, or rocking back and forth on your heels). Maintain good eye contact and do not under any circumstances look around the room for someone better to talk to. Many people look up or to the side when they are thinking; if you are one of those people, try to remember to look at the other person more often, otherwise they may think that you are disinterested.

ASK QUESTIONS

Don't talk about yourself too much, even if you think you have some really interesting stuff to tell people about yourself. If they only just met you they aren't really going to care unless they share the same interests. Instead, ask open-ended questions (those which cannot be answered with a simple "Yes" or "No"). Smile. In most cultures this is an essential way of showing interest and affability. Listen more than you talk.

Talking is always preferable to an embarrassed silence, so if you feel that the conversation is about to grind to a halt, ask another question, rather than wait in silence hoping that a better subject of conversation will pop into your mind.

PRACTICE ONLINE

Chatting online is a great way to practice making small talk, because it takes all visual clues such as body language and what you are wearing out of the situation and allows you to concentrate on what you are saying (or typing).

RELAX

It's not what you talk about that matters but how you talk: with confidence, interest, humor, warmth, and approachability. Don't worry about trying to appear intelligent or sexy or whatever (because you're only pandering to your own vanity anyway). Most strangers respond best to someone who is friendly and comfortable in their own skin.

Above all, don't worry about what other people are thinking of you. This frees you up to show an interest in them, rather than wasting time trying to leave a good impression.

SHAVE PROPERLY

A satisfying shave can never be rushed, and uses only the highest quality equipment (electricity not required). Use your daily shave as an opportunity to slow down, breathe slowly, and pamper yourself. Not only will this calm you down but it will also give you a better shave, with fewer nicks, because the worst thing you can do when shaving, apart from using a blunt razor, is to rush matters. Shave directly after a taking a bath or shower, while the stubble is at its softest.

SHAVING CREAM

Mass-market shaving foams or gels are adequate, but they ignore the dazzling luxury of fragrant and soothing shaving creams. Experience a high quality shaving cream just once and you'll never go back to foam in a can. Use a warm shaving bowl and a handmade badger-hair shaving brush (which range in stiffness from soft to hard, so choose one to your taste) to create a rich cream capable of locking maximum moisture into your beard.

Fill the bowl with hot water and leave for five minutes. Then tip out the water and place a blob of shaving cream the size of an almond onto your brush. Feather the brush around the bowl using a motion that is somewhere between a stir and a whisk, to work up a rich, creamy lather. Add a few drops of water while you whisk if the lather becomes too dry, then apply to your face using the brush. More skillful shavers work up the lather directly onto their beard without using a bowl. A warm bowl, however, gives the added pleasure of a warm lather that opens your pores and feels refreshing.

UNDER PRESSURE

Whether you are using a safety razor or a disposable plastic razor, the key to a close shave without nicks or razor burn, aside from the cream, is how hard you press the razor onto your face. A safety razor is much heavier than a disposable razor, so its own weight should add sufficient pressure. A disposable razor will need slightly more pressure that should still be fairly light.

SHORT AND SWEET

A common mistake is to try to remove too much hair in one stroke. Use short strokes and several passes. That way you are also less likely to clog the blade with hair. Rinse regularly to keep the blade clean.

SAFETY RAZORS

An old-fashioned safety razor is cheaper than a high-end disposable razor and will give you the best shave. To find the correct angle, hold the razor so that the handle is parallel to the floor; slowly move the razor down your face, and bring your arm down to decrease the angle. When the blade is about 30 degrees from perpendicular it will begin to cut through the hairs. This is the correct angle. Use short strokes and vary the angle to adjust to the contours of your face and chin.

If your skin is a bit saggy, pull it tightly upward using your free hand, just above the point where you are shaving. Shave downward (shaving upward removes too much skin and will leave you feeling sore).

AFTERCARE

After your shave, press a hot, damp towel against your face to open up your pores, then rinse with cold water, pat dry, and apply a small amount of moisturizer.

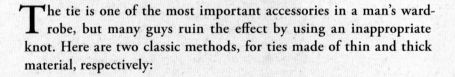

TIE A TIE

The tie is one of the most important accessories in a man's wardrobe, but many guys ruin the effect by using an inappropriate knot. Here are two classic methods, for ties made of thin and thick material, respectively:

FULL WINDSOR

Less attention-getting than the full monty but also less likely to get you arrested, the full Windsor is the emperor of all knots. Full and symmetrical, it projects stylish professionalism and is best suited to a long tie made of thin material (e.g., printed silk).

1. Drape the tie around your neck with the wide end on the side of your dominant hand (e.g., on the right if you're right-handed) and with the seam facing inward.

2. Locate the seam that goes diagonally across the front of the thin end, and pass the thick end over the thin end at this point (Fig. A). This ensures that the finished tie will be the correct length.

3. Pass the wide end up through the middle of the loop (Fig. B).

4. Bring the wide end to the right, pass it under the knot (seam facing upward), and then over the left side and down into the loop (Fig. C).

5. Bring the wide end around to the right again, pass it across the top of the knot (seam facing inward), and thread it down through the knot (Fig. D).

6. Tighten the knot by holding the narrow end of the tie and sliding the knot up to your neck (Fig. E).

Fig. A

Fig. B

Fig. C

Fig. D

Fig. E

FOUR HAND KNOT

This narrow knot is suitable for ties made from thicker material (e.g., woven silk), but it is less symmetrical than the Windsor.

1. Drape the tie around your neck with the thin end on the right-hand side (seam facing inward) and the wide end about eight inches below the thin end.

2. Take the wide end in your right hand and cross it over the thin end (seam facing inward) (Fig. A), then bring it back to the left side of your chest (seam facing outward) (Fig. B).

3. Bring the wide end to the right so that it crosses the top of the thin end again (seam facing inward) (Fig. C).

4. Pass the wide end up through the loop (Fig. D) and feed it down through the front knot (Fig. E).

5. Tighten the knot by holding the narrow end and sliding the knot up to your neck (Fig. F).

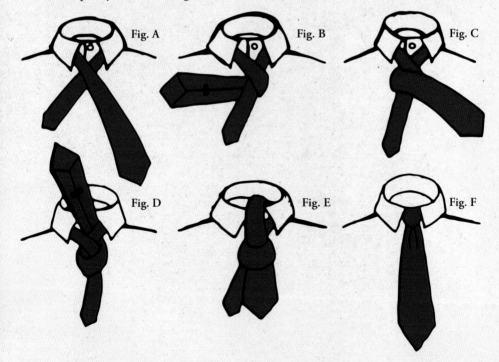

Fig. A   Fig. B   Fig. C

Fig. D   Fig. E   Fig. F

TIE TIPS

- To undo a tie, don't just loosen the knot and pull the tie over your head, as this will damage the fabric. Instead, pull the thin end through and clear of the knot, and the knot will fall apart easily.

- Always buy ties that are 100 percent silk, handmade, and properly lined. Avoid polyester and other synthetic materials. Obnoxious ties patterned with cartoon characters and other novelty features should be avoided at all costs. Trust us—they're not cute.

"I've found that you don't need to wear a necktie if you can hit."

—*Ted Williams, professional baseball player*

WISE MEN SAY

SURVIVE AN ANIMAL ATTACK

If you were attacked by a bear, mountain lion, crocodile, shark, or even man's best friend, would you know when to play dead and when to fight back? Here's how to increase your chances of survival in five life-or-death situations:

BEAR

Bear attacks are quite uncommon, but if you are approached by a bear, do not run. Leave any food you are carrying on the ground and walk away. If the bear continues to advance, stand and face it, place your hands on your hips, and make yourself look as big as possible. If the bear attacks you, lie on the ground, protect your face and neck with your hands and arms, and play dead. The bear's usual diet is fish and berries; a human is not its natural prey, so it will probably lose interest. If you fight back, however, the bear will reciprocate your aggression and kill you.

MOUNTAIN LION

Minimize the chances of attack by traveling in groups when hiking in cougar country. If you do encounter one of these big cats, don't crouch, bend over, or run away—these movements might trigger a chase response. Hold your ground, maintain eye contact, and try to look as intimidating as possible. Pick up any small children with you. If you are attacked, do NOT play dead. Fight back with all the speed and aggression you can muster. Use any weapon you can get your hands on: rocks, sticks, pepper spray, even a pen.

CROCODILE

Crocodiles kill hundreds of people every year. Avoid crocodile attacks by staying at least fifteen feet away from them on land, and farther away in the water. During a land attack, simply run away in a straight line (rather than a zigzag) as quickly as possible; the croc is unlikely to give chase unless you are running toward water. If you are attacked, fight back, aiming for the eyes, nostrils, and ears in that order of priority. If you are in the water and your arm or leg gets stuck in the croc's mouth, try to pull down the palatal valve just behind the tongue, and the croc will start swallowing water and let you go.

SHARK

Thankfully, shark attacks are rare. If you do encounter a shark, try to stay calm. If you can swim to shore, do so as smoothly as possible, keeping splashing to a minimum. If you are unable to get out of the water immediately, keep your eye on the shark, so you can be prepared if it attacks. If you are scuba diving, back up against a large rock, so you will only have to fend off a frontal attack. Do not play dead; fight back using all available weapons (speargun, camera, etc.). If nothing else, use your fists, elbows, knees, fingers, arms, and legs to inflict damage to the shark's head, especially the eyes and gills and the tip of its nose.

"To sit back hoping that someday, some way, someone will make things right is to go on feeding the crocodile, hoping he will eat you last—but eat you he will."

—*Ronald Reagan, former U.S. president*

WISE MEN SAY

DOG

Even the most docile mutt can become aggressive. The best way to avoid an attack is to recognize the warning signs. Do not pet or otherwise invade the personal space of a strange dog. A dog will turn its whole body away from you to show that it is not a threat. But if it feels threatened, it will lift its top lip and growl; the fur on its back (hackles) will stick up to make the dog appear bigger. This is the moment for you to back away slowly and avoid looking in its eyes. Its tail may be wagging vigorously, but this does not mean that you are safe. The dog may circle you before an attack, and will attack from behind if possible. Turn as it turns and continue facing it. Do not run away; the dog can outrun you. Speak slowly and calmly to the dog and say something like "Good boy" while avoiding eye contact.

If the dog attacks and knocks you to the ground, immediately curl into a ball, protect your face and neck with your hands and arms, and play dead, without making a sound. Screaming will only antagonize the dog further.

JUMPSTART A CAR

When your battery is dead, and you don't have time to wait for a tow truck, follow these twelve instructions to jumpstart your car using the battery of another vehicle.

1. Do not attempt to jumpstart a battery if the electrolyte solution inside is frozen or if the battery casing is cracked. Also, if the battery is dead because the car hasn't been used for several weeks, ventilate the area around the battery thoroughly to disperse any possible buildup of flammable hydrogen gas. You'll be glad you did.

2. Batteries contain sulfuric acid, so it's smart to wear protective gloves and eye goggles. Do not smoke or use an open flame near the engine. If it's dark, use a flashlight to see what you're doing.

3. Check that the batteries of both vehicles are of the same voltage. If not, the jumpstart won't work.

4. Park the source vehicle so that the jump cables will reach your battery, but make sure the cars do not actually touch. Turn off both ignitions.

5. To ensure good conductivity, use a knife or steel wool to remove any corrosion from the battery connectors.

6. It is vital that you connect and disconnect the jump leads in the correct order to avoid an explosion. Connect one end of the red jump lead to the positive terminal (marked POS or + and colored red) on the dead battery, then attach the other end of the same lead to the positive terminal on the source battery.

7. Next, connect one end of the black jump lead to the negative terminal (marked NEG or – and colored black) of the source battery, then attach the other end of the black jump lead to the metal engine block of the dead car, as far away from the battery as possible; this creates a ground.

8. Keep the red and black leads away from each other; if they touch they will cause a short circuit. Also, keep the leads away from the moving parts of each engine.

9. Start the engine of the source car first (this ensures that its battery won't die while you're attempting to start the other car), then turn the ignition key on the dead car. If it doesn't start, wait for about ten seconds and try again. If it still fails to start after several attempts, stop, otherwise you could damage the starter motor.

10. If the dead car starts, leave both cars running and remove the jump leads in the reverse order shown in steps 6 and 7.

"I bought some batteries, but they weren't included."

—*Steven Wright, stand-up comedian, actor, and author*

WISE MEN SAY

11. Even though your vehicle has started, your battery is still dead, so you need to drive around for at least half an hour to allow the alternator to partially recharge the battery (don't leave the engine running with the car stationary, as it could overheat). Only then should you switch off the engine.

12. Charge the battery overnight using a battery charger. In rare cases the battery can become so dead that it cannot be recharged. When this happens, replace it with a new one.

PROTECT YOURSELF DURING A LIGHTNING STORM

Lightning kills about a hundred people—and injures ten times as many—in the United States each year. If you can hear thunder, you are in danger, however slight, of being struck by lightning. Take these ten precautions to minimize your risk of being injured.

1. Stay away from trees (don't be tempted to take shelter underneath one) and isolated features such as lampposts, telephone poles, or radio towers.

2. You are relatively safe inside a car, as long as it has a metal roof and sides. If the car is struck by lightning, the metal will conduct the electricity around you, not through you.

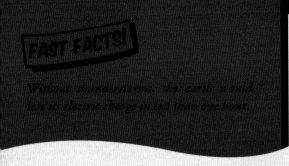
3. If you are swimming, get to dry land as quickly as possible and take cover indoors. If you are in a boat and cannot get to shore, stay in the boat instead of jumping into the water. When struck by lightning, a boat is a better place to be rendered unconscious than in the water. Crouch down in the center of the boat, well away from metal hardware.

4. Move from high ground to lower ground, unless you need to escape flooding.

5. If you are on a golf course, drop your metal clubs and head for the clubhouse.

6. Take cover indoors whenever possible, inside a substantial structure. Once inside keep all windows and external doors closed and stay within the inner rooms of the building. Use only a cordless telephone for emergencies; this is because the biggest cause of indoor lightning injuries is telephone use, as electricity can travel long distances down telephone as well as electrical wires. Cordless phones and cell phones are safe to use.

7. If a severe storm is approaching, unplug all electrical items from wall outlets, including telephones and modems. If your house or someplace nearby is struck by lightning, these items will short out. During a storm avoid touching electrical appliances and plumbing, stay away from doors and windows, and do not use the bath or shower. Do not stand on bare concrete or lean against bare concrete walls, as they may contain metal cables. Remain inside for at least thirty minutes after you see the last lightning strike.

8. If you can't get indoors, crouch down with your feet together, your head tucked into your chest, and your hands covering your ears. Avoid wide-open areas, because if you are the only significant feature in an otherwise open and featureless landscape, a lightning bolt will seek to ground itself through you! In other words, it will usually hit the tallest object.

9. If you are caught outside with a group of people spread out so that there are several body lengths between each person, and crouch down as described above. This reduces the chances of multiple casualties.

10. When someone has been struck by lightning, they are safe to touch (you will not get electrocuted). Call emergency services immediately, and administer CPR if their heart has stopped beating. Check for two major burns: the places where the electricity entered and exited the body.

THE 30/30 RULE

Count the time between a lightning strike and the thunder. If that time is thirty seconds or less, the thunderstorm is within six miles of you and is dangerous. You should seek shelter and remain protected for at least 30 minutes after you hear the last thunder clap.

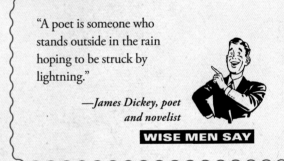

"A poet is someone who stands outside in the rain hoping to be struck by lightning."

—*James Dickey, poet and novelist*

WISE MEN SAY

ASK FOR A RAISE

G enerally, we all attract more or less what we think we are worth, and nowhere is this truer than in the workplace. Are you getting paid what you deserve? If not, it's time to stand up for yourself and demand what is rightfully yours.

CONFIDENCE

This is the most important element of success in any field. If you don't believe in your own worth (and that you deserve to be paid more for it), then how can you expect your boss to feel any differently? You need to be able to back up your case with hard facts, however, and this means being able to show how your actions have had positive results within your company, resulting in increased revenues and productivity, better communication, a wider client base, etc. If you can name ten ways in which you have brought value to the company, your boss will find it harder to say no to a raise. It also reminds you of how valuable you could be to another company if you don't get the desired results.

RESEARCH

Find out the salary range that is the norm within your profession and at your level, so that you neither under- nor oversell yourself. Ask colleagues within your company as well as outside what they understand the range to be (your corporate culture may well discourage this, but that's only to keep everyone in the dark). Check the recruitment section of newspapers and online to find out the salary range of equivalent jobs to yours. Also refer to online salary survey websites.

TIMING

Time your request carefully. Asking for a raise after there have just been wide-scale layoffs is not only futile but will actually damage your credibility; the best time is just after you've completed a project or have done something that has raised your profile positively.

BE FLEXIBLE

If your boss is unwilling to reward you financially, think creatively about other ways in which he can improve your overall package: more flexible working hours, better perks, options, etc. If you are already at the top of your pay scale, ask for additional responsibilities to justify a pay increase.

NEXT TIME

If you are turned down for a raise, make sure that your boss gives you an idea of how long it will be before she is prepared to reassess the situation: six months, a year, or longer? This not only keeps you on her mind but also gives you a clearer idea of your middle-term future prospects.

DO NOT . . .

➥ . . . give your boss a sob story about why you need the extra money. You are a professional, not a charity case, and what you do with your money is your business, not his.

❧ . . . demand to be given a raise in line with other named individuals in the company. Your boss will always be able to counter this rather indiscreet approach by pointing out mitigating circumstances such as length of service or skills differences. Focus on your own worth and what you bring to the table, rather than comparing yourself with others.

❧ . . . threaten to leave unless you have a guaranteed job offer elsewhere, otherwise you'll be out of a job if your bluff is called. Emphasize your loyalty to your company.

> "Your earning ability is largely determined by the perception of excellence, quality, and value that others have of you and what you do. The market only pays excellent rewards for excellent performance. It pays average rewards for average performance, and it pays below-average rewards or unemployment for below-average performance."
>
> —*Brian Tracy, author and motivational speaker*

> "Your needs will be met once you can find a way of projecting energy and fulfilling someone else's need."
>
> —*Stuart Wilde, self-help author*

WISE MEN SAY

AMAZE YOUR FRIENDS

We think that every guy should have a few tricks up his sleeve. Magic tricks don't have to be confined to the professionals—anyone can perfect them with a bit of knowledge and a little practice. These five tricks are simple to do but are sure to entertain your friends and family as they wonder how on earth you did it!

THE LOST ACE

Starting with a new pack of cards, remove the four aces and place them face-up on the table so that everyone can see. Hand the remaining cards to a friend and ask him to check that there are no other aces in the pack. Then pick up the four aces from the table and ask the friend to shuffle them into the pack.

Ask the friend if he is sure he has all the aces in his possession. He will, of course, say yes. Next, reach into your pocket and produce the ace of diamonds. When the friend inspects the pack, he will find that this card is missing. How'd you do it?

SECRET: Before the trick hide the ace of diamonds in your pocket; use the nine of diamonds for the ace, but when you lay them on the table make sure the other aces are covering all but the central diamond. With a little practice this can be done in an apparently careless manner of arranging the cards on the table, and finally placing the last ace over them.

BANANA SPLIT

Did you know that bananas have five sides? Count them and see! Now here's a fruity way to baffle banana lovers everywhere!

•◦ You will need a banana, a sewing needle, and some thread.

•◦ Thread a clean needle with thread. Starting at one end, push the needle through the banana skin at one of its corners and out again at the next corner. Repeat all the way around until you're back where you started. Hold both ends of the thread and gently pull. This will slice the banana without breaking the skin! Repeat five more times in different places.

•◦ When the banana is peeled it will fall apart into seven slices. You've made a magic banana split!

FREE FALL

Here's how to be flush without spending a penny!

•◦ Place a quarter on the floor, a foot away from a wall.

•◦ Tell your friend he can have the money. All he has to do is stand with his back and heels touching the wall, feet flat on the floor, and bend over to pick up the gift!

•◦ After he's tried and failed a few times, pick up the coin and say, "Well, if you don't want it . . ." and walk away.

It's impossible to bend over like that without sticking your backside out—but your friend can't because the wall is in the way!

NOSE JOB
This is a simple way to fake a dislocated nose. Put your hands together and place them over your nose and mouth. Sharply snap your hands from side to side while clicking your top teeth with your thumbnails. A sickening "crack" will convince onlookers that you need an urgent nose splint!

HIGHLY STRUNG
How long is a piece of string? It's longer than you think, as this simple trick demonstrates.

➤ Thread a long piece of string through your sweater or shirt, so that only a little bit is sticking out. Hide the rest in a ball or on a bobbin inside your clothing. Someone is sure to notice the thread and give it a tug. But they'll end up with more than they bargained for!

DEFEND YOURSELF IN A FIST FIGHT

Most of us haven't put up our dukes since we left high school, but even if you aren't the sort of guy who goes looking for a rumble, you never know when you'll need to defend yourself. And if you do find yourself in a sticky situation, a little knowledge and practice can make the difference between taking a pounding and walking away in better shape than your attacker. Note that we used the word "attacker," because the only time you should fight is if it is unavoidable. Remember that the best way to "win" a fight is to get the other guy to cool it or walk away. Don't let him rattle your cage.

ESTABLISH YOUR SAFETY ZONE

If the other guy is cruising for a bruising and seems to be getting increasingly frosted, make sure to keep him at arm's length. Keep backing away; if he follows, keep him outside your "safety zone"—at least three feet away from you.

TAKE A DEFENSIVE STANCE

Hold your hands up at chest height; outstretch one slightly bent arm as a shield or guard between you and your attacker. If he touches this hand, strike. Once someone enters your safety zone they mean business, and you have no alternative but to get in the first knuckle sandwich.

YOUR FIRST MOVE

Slam your outstretched hand—with the hand open—into his face. This will more than likely stop any punches he is also throwing, no sweat. A simple hand in the face will disorient most people considerably.

KNUCKLE SANDWICH, SERVED COLD

Your two main strikes should be with punches and low kicks. For punches, keep your hand, wrist, and two big knuckles in a straight line, and punch with those two knuckles.

- Hit as hard and as fast as you can, without dropping your guard, landing as many punches as possible in a short time.

- Don't curve your punches; punch in a straight line and aim past the target, so that when your fist makes contact you will follow through. Don't stop on the target—this is called pulling your punch.

IF WORSE COMES TO WORST

- Assume that you will get hit; don't be shocked when this happens, just keep fighting. Don't hold your breath; stay calm and focused even though the blood and adrenaline will be pumping through your body.

- If you can see a punch coming but are unable to get out of the way, duck your head, so that you take the punch with your forehead instead of your neck, nose, or jaw. Keep your mouth shut and your tongue well inside it, but don't clench your teeth.

- If you end up wrestling, your best chance is to get him on the floor before he does it to you, so that you have the advantage. Knees and elbows can be used close up, as well as head butts and upper cuts.

- Remember, street fighting can get ugly. It's not a boxing match—it's about getting out in one piece. Using reasonable force, do whatever it takes to stop your opponent from fighting you. The fight ends when he stops fighting or cuts out, not before.

FORECAST
THE WEATHER

If you want to know what to wear tomorrow, there are several simple techniques that can help you to predict the weather. They aren't foolproof, but then neither are the multimillion-dollar computerized weather-prediction systems used by the world's top meteorologists.

CLOUD PATTERNS

Check out the shapes of the clouds. If they are fluffy, like big cotton balls, the weather is settled. If the clouds are rising, the weather will get better. If the clouds take any shape other than fluffy balls, it means that bad weather may be imminent. The following cloud behaviors are all signs that the weather is going to get worse:

- More clouds are forming, especially at low to medium altitudes.

- Clouds are getting thicker and darker.

- Clouds are growing taller and blacker at the base.

- Clouds are rushing across the sky or moving in several different directions.

- On a hot day, clouds forming in the afternoon from water that has evaporated from the ground during the day may bring rain and possibly storms.

- Fluffy clouds piled one on top of the other may bring sudden downpours.

- If thin and wispy (cirrus) clouds start to join up or thicken, rain is on the way during the next forty-eight hours.

EVENING AND MORNING SKY

Check the morning and evening sky. A red sky at night indicates good weather tomorrow. The sun sets in the west, so a red sunset means that you are looking at clear weather to the west. Because weather systems usually move from west to east, this indicates that clearer weather is on the way. A red sky in the morning means clouds to the west, which may mean rain is on the way.

SUN AND MOON

If the halo surrounding the moon or sun begins to shrink, this is a good indicator that the cloud cover is thickening; expect rain within twelve hours.

"Sunshine is delicious, rain is refreshing, wind braces us up, snow is exhilarating; there is really no such thing as bad weather, only different kinds of good weather."

—*John Ruskin, critic, author, poet, and artist*

"The trouble with weather forecasting is that it's right too often for us to ignore it and wrong too often for us to rely on it."

—*Patrick Young, visual artist*

WISE MEN SAY

PLANTS AND ANIMALS

Many plants close their flowers before rain. When animals are settled, so is the weather. When animals become unsettled or agitated, it is usually a sign that bad weather is imminent, or that a storm is brewing. When farm animals stay around trees or low-lying shelters, rain may be close, but if they climb to high ground expect fair weather.

BUY A BAROMETER

Your parents and grandparents probably have one of these; it measures atmospheric pressure. Generally, high pressure brings settled weather and low pressure brings rain.

RUN A MARATHON

A marathon is 26.2 miles long, and requires a lot of preparation in order to make running it an injury-free and semi-enjoyable experience. In other words, you can't just wake up one morning and decide to run a marathon. You need at least a year of running experience and training behind you. If you currently don't run at all but want to start working up to marathon fitness, spend several weeks walking a few miles briskly every day to ease yourself into it.

SHOES

Find the right pair of sneakers. Go to a small specialist sports shop, where you are more likely to receive expert advice and fitting than you would at a large outlet. Choose sneakers specifically designed for running (rather than those made to be fashion accessories or designed for other sports). If you have an old pair of sneakers, bring them with you when you buy a new pair, so that the fitter can examine the wear pattern and tailor the fitting more closely to your individual needs. Use your new sneakers only for running, otherwise they will wear out more quickly and develop adverse wear patterns.

CLOTHING

Wear layers in cold weather, and loose, light-colored clothes and a cap to keep you cool during the summer and to protect you from sunburn. Buy a watch with a stopwatch function so you can time your progress.

DIET

The quality and quantity of the fuel you put into your body has a direct result on your energy output. Eat meals that are high in carbohydrates and low in fat, as well as lean proteins such as fish and chicken. Eat at least five portions each of fruit and vegetables a day and drink plenty of water. While you are training you will need to drink a minimum of four quarts of water each day. Eat a small snack and drink a glass of water about half an hour before each training session. Eat a large bowl of pasta the night before the big race to load up on carbs (this maximizes the amount of glycogen in your muscles).

"The truth is that every runner in a marathon is a survivor or nothing, including the winner."

—*Dr. George Sheehan,*
cardiologist, runner, and author

WISE MEN SAY

TRAINING

Consult a doctor for a medical checkup before you begin training. Build up your distance and speed gradually during your training and never run more than 10 percent farther than you did the previous week, to avoid injury and overtraining. Start walking/running at least a year before the marathon; begin to follow the program outlined below twenty-six weeks before the race.

MARATHON TRAINING PROGRAM

Each week consists of five run days (one long and four shorter) and two rest days. Good training puts stress on various components of the body, so that it is pushed beyond its current limits but not so much that you sustain an injury.

Week	Long run (1 day/wk)	Shorter runs (4 days/wk)
Weeks 1–2	Run 4 miles	2–4 miles
Weeks 3–4	Run 6 miles	4–5 miles
Weeks 5–6	Run 8 miles	4–6 miles
Weeks 7–8	Run 10 miles	4–6 miles
Weeks 9–10	Run 11 miles	5–8 miles
Weeks 11–12	Run 12 miles	5–8 miles
Weeks 13–14	Run 14 miles	6–8 miles
Weeks 15–16	Run 16 miles	6–8 miles
Weeks 17–18	Run 10 miles	4–5 miles
Weeks 19–20	Run 16 miles	6–8 miles
Weeks 21–22	Run 16 miles	6–8 miles
Weeks 23–24	Run 14 miles	6–8 miles
Week 25	Run 10 miles	4–8 miles
Week 26	Run 3 miles every other day	

WARMING UP

It is important to stretch all the muscle groups in your back, arms, and legs before and after a training session. Don't make the mistake of running too fast and exhausting yourself quickly, otherwise you will quickly feel unmotivated. If you are training with a partner, run at a pace that allows you to talk comfortably. Also, allow yourself to walk for a couple of minutes when you feel that you can't run another step. If you are unable to run fifteen miles comfortably three weeks before the race you should pull out.

THE BIG RACE

Don't buy a new pair of sneakers; use the ones you've been training with! Drink as much water as you can during the race. Rest up for a week afterward.

RIDE A HORSE

T here was a time when every man knew his way around a horse. For better or worse, those days are behind us. Still, we believe that every guy should know the basics of horsemanship, if only because horse-riding is such pleasure. No ride is ever quite the same as the next, but anyone can learn how to do it. All it takes is plenty of patience and a sense of humor. Here are the basics:

MOUNTING WITHOUT TEARS

Hold the reins in your left hand and grasp the bottom of the horse's mane with the same hand. Hold the left stirrup in your right hand so you can guide your left foot into it. Grasping the back of the saddle with your right hand, push off on the ball of your right foot, and hoist yourself up with your arms so that all of your weight is on the left foot in the stirrup. Now swing your right leg over the horse's back, lower yourself into the saddle, and place your right foot in the other stirrup.

RIDING POSITION

Sit in the lowest part of the saddle, and open your hips so that your heels are in line with them. Keep your upper body straight, and face forward. Hold the reins such that your thumbs and little fingers are under the reins and the other fingers are curled over the reins, so that your thumb is on top and your knuckles are facing forward.

WALKING

To make a horse walk, squeeze gently with your lower legs, then relax them once the horse has started to move. If this doesn't work, give the horse a gentle kick with both heels to get it going. Allow your hands to move back and forth in time with the nodding movement of the horse's head, so that the reins are kept at the same state of tension.

TROTTING

Make a horse trot by squeezing slightly harder with your lower legs, or give a gentle kick with your heels. When a horse trots it does not bob its head, so you won't need to compensate with your hands. You will need, however, to push your hips upward and forward in a gentle thrusting movement in time with the horse's gait. This makes your bottom sit and rise rhythmically in and out of the saddle, in what is called a rising trot. Alternatively, you can assume a "sitting trot" that uses the same movements, except that your bottom stays in the saddle, but you have to make sure you keep your legs and back relaxed as you bounce.

CANTERING AND GALLOPING

While you are in a sitting trot you can ask a horse to canter by moving one of your legs back slightly and then squeezing gently with both legs. As with walking, the horse will bob its head as it canters, so you will need to move your hands back and forth to maintain equal tension in the reins. Keep your back soft and supple and allow your hips to rock in time with the canter. If your back is stiff, both you and the horse will feel considerable discomfort. Push

"There is something about the outside of a horse that is good for the inside of a man."

—*Winston Churchill,
Prime Minister of the United
Kingdom from 1940 to 1945*

WISE MEN SAY

your horse into the gallop from the canter in the same way.

TURNING

A rider turns a horse by using the reins and his legs. To turn a horse left, gently pull back on the left rein, making the horse bend its neck to the left, and apply pressure with your legs to encourage the horse to continue forward. To turn a horse to the right, gently pull back on the right rein, making the horse bend its neck to the right. Move the opposite leg back slightly (i.e., right leg on a left turn; left leg on a right turn) to help guide the horse on a gentle curve.

SLOWING DOWN AND STOPPING

Stiffen your lower back, squeeze gently with your legs, and pull the reins back gently. As soon as the horse has obeyed your request, release the leg and rein pressure.

DISMOUNTING

When the horse is stationary, hold the reins with your left hand and place both hands on the front of the saddle. Straighten your legs so that you are standing up in the stirrups, then swing your right leg backward over the horse's quarters as you move your right hand to the back of the saddle. Kick your left foot out of the stirrup and push back slightly as you drop gracefully to the ground.

BRAIN FOOD

A man rode into town on Friday. He stayed for three nights and then left on Friday. How?

Solution: Friday is the name of the horse.

FINDING DIRECTIONS WITHOUT A COMPASS

When you are well and truly lost and you don't have a compass, nature can provide you with lots of ways to find your bearings; the sun, moon, stars, and even trees can give you a sense of direction.

CLIMB UP HIGH

Get yourself to some high ground so that you can survey the terrain from a good vantage point. Draw a simple map showing key features such as rivers, mountains, trees, etc., so that you won't have to rely solely on your memory. Then use some of the methods below to find N, S, E and W and mark them on your map.

RISING AND SETTING SUN

The sun can give you directions, so long as you know what time it is. In the northern hemisphere the sun rises in the east and sets in the west. When it reaches its highest point at noon, its direction is true south in the northern hemisphere (and north in the southern hemisphere).

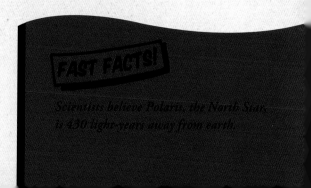
MOON

At dusk if the moon rises before the sun sets, the illuminated side is west; if it rises after dark, the illuminated side is east.

THE NORTH STAR

On a clear night in the northern hemisphere, locate Polaris, the North Star. It is at the end of the "handle" in the constellation known as Ursa Minor (the Little Dipper or Little Bear), which is just above Ursa Major (The Big Dipper or Great Bear). If you draw a line from the 2 stars in the handle of the Big Dipper, upwards, it will reach Polaris. Walk towards Polaris and you will be heading north.

TREES

There are fewer branches on the north face of a tree than on the south, and it is wetter, so there will also be more mosses on the north face. If you spot an ants' nest against a tree, it will usually be on the south side.

MAKE A NATURAL COMPASS

If the sky is clear and there is plenty of sunshine, this method is reasonably accurate, but time consuming. Find a straight stick or pole about a yard long and stick it vertically into the ground where the terrain is flat, in the morning. The stick casts a shadow. Place a marker (small stick/

stone) at the exact spot where the shadow ends. Every 20 minutes mark the new place where the shadow ends.

During the day the shadow will move and grow shorter and longer. At noon the shadow will be at its shortest—make a special mark at this point—and it will be pointing due north (or south if you are in the southern hemisphere). If you can't wait that long, wait for 20 minutes and draw a line between the two shadow ends. It will be roughly west-east (because the shadow will always move west to east). Stand facing the line with the first mark on your left and you'll be facing north.

"Stand still. The trees ahead and bush beside you are not lost."

—*Albert Einstein, Nobel Prize-winning physicist*

"Walking isn't a lost art -- one must, by some means, get to the garage."

—*Evan Esar, humorist*

WISE MEN SAY

SMOKE A CIGAR

There is more to smoking a cigar than inhaling and exhaling. In fact, stop right there if you can't see anything wrong with that last sentence: didn't you know that you should NEVER inhale smoke from a cigar? Sit back in your Chesterfield chair, pull on your smoking jacket, and read on to appreciate the subtleties of enjoying a premium stogie.

CHOOSING A CIGAR

The best cigars in the world are the big fat Havanas, but these are difficult to acquire as well as very expensive. Also, if you are a cigar novice, it is best to start off with a thinner cigar, as it will be easier to light. When you are more experienced you can increase the length and diameter of your cigars; it's generally the case that the thicker and longer the cigar, the smoother and richer the flavor and the cooler the smoke.

Test the quality of the cigar by squeezing it slightly to make sure there are no lumps. The color should be uniform. Don't buy a cigar that has a discolored wrapper. Make sure the cigar is 100 percent tobacco.

CIGAR TYPES

Cigars come in many sizes and shapes, and they are described in terms of their diameter and length. The diameter is the ring gauge (for example, a Churchill has a 47 ring gauge, or 47/64ths of an inch). Here are some common cigar types:

CHURCHILL Long and thick with straight sides, this cigar was named for Winston Churchill. It is usually about 7 inches long with a 47 gauge.

LONSDALE Long with straight sides, the Lonsdale is usually about 7 inches long and has a medium gauge of 44.

FIGURADA This is the name for any cigar that doesn't have parallel or straight sides. These include the Torpedo, which has a pointed head, closed foot, and a bulge in the middle; the Pyramid, which has a pointed, closed head; and the Perfecto, with two closed ends and a bulge in the middle.

ROBUSTO Typically 5 inches in length with a 50 ring gauge, these short, fat stogies are sometimes called Bullies or Rothchilds.

CUTTING IT

In Westerns and gangster movies, the tough guys bite off the ends of their cigars and spit them at the nearest stray dog. This, however, is frowned upon in polite society, and will decrease the pleasure of the cigar, as the head must be removed with a clean, horizontal cut to release the maximum flavor.

To do this properly, use a single-bladed cutter to remove the head at the point where the cap of the cigar meets the wrapper. Try not to tear the wrapper, and remove the band only after the cigar has been lit (its purpose is to prevent the tobacco from tearing).

LIGHTING IT

The way you light your cigar has a significant impact on its taste. Avoid matches and kerosene lighters, as the chemicals (sulphur and ammonia) will sully the delicate aroma of the cigar. Instead, use a lighter filled with odorless butane, or a wooden spill (a thin strip of wood, usually cedar). Angle the cigar at no more than 30 degrees below horizontal, otherwise you will suck up soot through the end of the cigar.

Hold the flame against the end of the cigar, rotating it slowly to light the entire rim, otherwise it will burn unevenly. Then put it in your mouth. Holding the cigar horizontally, touch the flame to the very tip and draw on it slowly as you continue to rotate. If your cigar is well made, it will burn evenly and develop a firm, even ash while you're smoking.

"Happiness? A good cigar, a good meal, a good cigar, and a good woman—or a bad woman; it depends on how much happiness you can handle."

—*George Burns, vaudevillian, radio personality, and actor*

"If I cannot smoke cigars in heaven I shall not go!"

—*Mark Twain, author and satirist*

WISE MEN SAY

DELIVER A SPEECH

Though some people are naturally better orators than others, any-one can learn how to speak in public as long as they prepare prop-erly and manage to stay relaxed.

PRACTICE MAKES PERFECT

If you want to connect powerfully with your audience, you'll need to allow plenty of time to rehearse your speech. Even if you don't need to memorize the speech, you should know the material thoroughly, so that when you speak the words and ideas will sound fresh and unrehearsed. Familiarity with your material also allows you to speak with greater conviction. Understand the purpose of your speech and summarize it for yourself in a sentence.

YOU AND YOUR AUDIENCE

When you deliver your speech, imagine you are talking to a large group of friends. Not only will this help to calm your nerves, it will also allow you to be more yourself and to develop a conversational style. Imagine you are talking to individual people who like and admire you, rather than to a sea of hostile faces.

Make brief eye contact—about three seconds—with individual members of your audience; don't just talk to one section of it, or over people's heads as you stare at the back wall. Many of us stiffen up when we are talking to a large group when we should be doing the opposite: opening up and allowing our personality to be expressed naturally and unselfconsciously. Remember that everyone in the audience wants you to succeed. Don't show your anxiety, and never apologize for it (confessing to your audience that you're nervous will likely make the situation only more awkward for everyone).

DON'T FORGET TO BREATHE

Many of us take quick, shallow breaths when we are nervous. People who speak for a living, such as actors, have learned how to breathe more slowly and deeply from their stomach, rather than their chest (not literally, of course). This does wonders for calming the jitters. To practice deep breathing, place your hand on your stomach and relax your chest. As you breathe slowly and deeply, try to make your stomach—not your chest—go in and out. When your breath is well supported in this way it also becomes easier to vary the speed, volume, and pitch of your voice. Learn the value of the pause, which allows thinking and reflection, and always try to use humor whenever it is appropriate and possible.

"Be sincere; be brief; be seated."

*—Franklin D. Roosevelt,
former U.S. president*

"Once you get people laughing, they're listening, and you can tell them almost anything."

*—Herbert Gardner,
comedian and banker*

WISE MEN SAY

BUILD A FIRE

To build a fire you need tinder and kindling; to light a fire you need a spark and plenty of oxygen. Sounds easy, doesn't it? First, let's look at ways to build a fire, then we will learn how to light it without the benefit of matches.

TINDER

Tinder is highly flammable material that is used to ignite your kindling. Ideally, it should catch fire easily after making contact with a spark, so above all it needs to be dry. You can use lots of different materials for tinder: dry grasses, dry bark (especially cedar or birch), moss, bulrush seeds, or dried "tinder fungus," a fungus that grows in black clumps on live birch trees. The finer and drier the tinder, the easier it will be to ignite.

When searching for tinder in wet conditions look on the underside of dead wood for dry "punk" wood that has decomposed to form a powdery material. The thin, brittle branches of a dead tree will usually burn, even under the wettest conditions. Or you can use manmade tinder such as wax-coated cardboard or cotton balls coated with petroleum jelly.

KINDLING

Kindling is flammable material that is denser than tinder but requires greater heat to ignite, which is why your fire requires sufficient tinder so that the kindling begins to burn independently and can then act as the main source of fuel for the fire. Twigs and sticks are the most obvious and abundant source of kindling, but you can also use tree bark, wood chips and shavings, and even feathers.

BUILDING THE FIRE

Once you have gathered all of your tinder and kindling you are ready to build a structure for your fire. Different structures are suited for different materials and purposes. Here are four common fire-building methods:

TEPEE Arrange the kindling around the tinder to make the shape of a conical tepee, with the sticks forming an apex at the top. Place the thinnest sticks on the inside of the tepee and the thickest sticks and logs on the outside. As the fire burns, the sticks and logs will fall inward and feed the fire. This method works well with damp wood, because the heat of the fire can help to dry out the external wood before it burns.

CROSS-DITCH Dig a cross shape in the ground about a foot wide and about three inches deep. Place a ball of tinder in the center of the cross and build a kindling tepee over the top. As the tinder and kindling burn, air is drawn into the ditch to provide oxygen at the base of the fire.

LEAN-TO Drive a long stick into the ground at a 30-degree angle to horizontal, with the point of the stick facing into the wind. Lay kindling sticks against the lean-to stick in increasing size order to form a rooflike structure that is open at one end. Place the tinder into this structure, where the lean-to stick enters the ground. As the fire burns add more kindling as required.

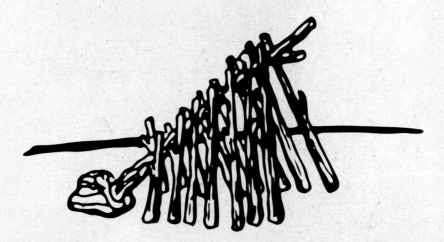

PYRAMID Place two small logs on the ground parallel to each other. Place a layer of shorter logs across the first two logs, as if you were building a raft; then place three or four layers of increasingly shorter logs, each at right angles to the one beneath, until you have a pyramid shape. Place kindling and tinder at the top of the pyramid and light it. As this fire burns it will ignite the logs below it. The advantage of this sort of fire is that it does not need further attention, so it can burn through the night.

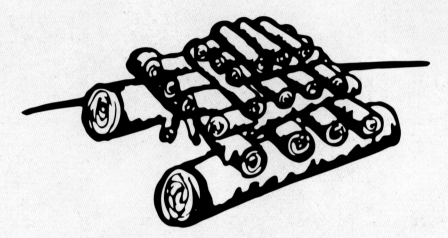

LIGHTING YOUR FIRE

If you're stuck without matches or a cigarette lighter, you can use a convex lens such as a magnifying glass to focus the sun's rays onto the tinder, or strike a flint against a piece of metal to create a spark. Failing this, you can build a wooden fire plow to create a spark using friction. Cut a straight groove into a piece of soft wood, then rub a pointed hardwood stick rapidly up and down the groove to generate a small pile of sawdust and wood fibers. Tip the "coal" onto your tinder and blow gently until the tinder smokes and finally—hopefully—bursts into flame.

CARVE A TURKEY

While you might not serve a whole roast turkey more than a few times a year, knowing the proper carving technique will amaze your friends and relatives.

→ Remove the turkey from the oven, cover with aluminum foil, and leave for fifteen minutes before carving. This allows the meat to relax, making it juicier, more tender, and easier to carve. Use a sharp carving knife and a long carving fork. Once it has rested, transfer the turkey, breast-side-up, to a carving board. Now it's ready to be carved.

- Remove the legs by pulling each leg away from the body using one hand or the flat side of the knife. Locate the joint where the leg attaches to the backbone and cut through it (don't try to cut through bone) and the skin.

- Place each leg on a cutting board and cut through the joint to separate the thigh from the leg. Either serve the drumstick whole or tilt it slightly and remove the meat by slicing downward, turning the drumstick to get slices of equal size (make sure you remove the hard tendons). For the thigh, either serve it intact or cut several slices downward and parallel to the bone.

- Remove the wings by cutting through the joint where the wing meets the body.

- To carve the breast meat, first make a deep cut into the breast along the body just above and parallel to the wing. Then carve thin slices downward from the middle of the breast; the slices will fall away when your knife reaches the first deep cut.

- Alternatively, you may choose to remove the whole breast and then carve it (the "kitchen method"). Separate each breast lobe from the rib cage by cutting along the keel bone and around the body. Place the breast on a cutting board and slice it against the grain of the meat.

➤ Carve only as much meat as is required for the first serving, to prevent the meat from drying out. Also, cut the dark meat first (leg, thigh), as it will stay moist longer than the white meat (breast).

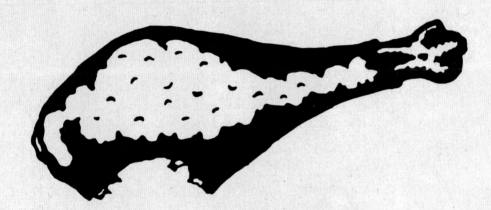

"I hate turkeys. If you stand in the meat section at the grocery store long enough, you start to get mad at turkeys. There's turkey ham, turkey bologna, turkey pastrami. Someone needs to tell the turkey, man, just be yourself."

—*Mitch Hedberg, stand-up comedian*

"I wish the bald eagle had not been chosen as the representative of our country. He is a bird of bad moral character … Like those among men who live by sharking and robbing, he is generally poor, and often very lousy … The turkey in comparison is a much more respectable bird."

—*Benjamin Franklin, scientist, inventor, statesman, printer, and author*

WISE MEN SAY

FIX A FLAT TIRE

Your Driver's Ed teachers were right —you really should know what to do if you hear that dreaded flapping sound of a flat when cruising along the highway. It's great to have AAA, but if your cell phone has no service or if you're in another country, you'll be glad you're self-sufficient.

1. Park the car on flat, stable ground, and away from passing traffic, if possible. Set the handbrake and put the car into first gear (or Park in an automatic). Make sure that all of the car's passengers leave the vehicle and stand at a safe distance away from oncoming traffic. For added security, place a brick underneath the wheel diagonally opposite the flat tire, and if

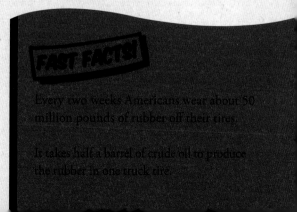

FAST FACTS!

Every two weeks Americans wear about 50 million pounds of rubber off their tires.

It takes half a barrel of crude oil to produce the rubber in one truck tire.

the ground is soft place a solid board underneath the jack.

2. If you keep an orange cone in your trunk, place it ten feet behind your car to warn passing motorists. Turn on your hazard lights. Get the spare tire, wheel brace, and jack from the trunk.

3. If you have a hubcap (rather than an alloy wheel), remove it with a screwdriver or the end of the wheel brace, and use it to hold the nuts after they have been removed.

4. Use the wheel brace to loosen the nuts, diagonally opposite each other (usually you have to turn them counterclockwise, unless the nut has an "R" on it). If one of the nuts is a "locking nut" (to prevent wheel theft), locate the locking-nut key (which is often kept with the wheel brace or in the glove compartment). You must fit the key onto the end of the wheel brace before you attempt to turn the locking nut. If the nuts are stiff you may have to use your foot.

5. Look for a sturdy place to position the end of the jack, such as on the frame of the car next to the flat tire but not on the flimsy bodywork. When in doubt, consult your car manual for the correct placement. Turn the handle of the jack until it meets the frame.

6. Jack up the car until the flat tire is about six inches clear of the ground. Leave enough space so that the new tire (which will need more clearance than the flat tire) can be comfortably slid into place.

7. Do not put any part of your body underneath the car or tire. The jack could slip, causing the car to fall on you.

8. Unscrew the nuts and remove them. Pull the tire horizontally toward you to slide it away and off the car. Insert the spare tire onto the threaded bolts and push it until it won't go any farther. Tighten the nuts (diagonally) as much as possible.

9. Let the jack down so that all four wheels are in contact with the ground, then tighten the nuts completely, working with pairs of diagonal opposites. Lower the car completely, remove the jack, and tighten the nuts for the final time. Replace the hubcap.

10. Visit your garage at the earliest opportunity to repair the flat tire or to get a replacement. Some spare tires are not designed to be used for a long period of time; in any case, the garage will need to rebalance your wheels.

MAKE A GREAT FIRST IMPRESSION

We know you've heard it a thousand times, but here we go again: you never get a second chance to make a great first impression. The best way to make a great first impression is to convey confidence without being overbearing. Relaxation is the key to mastering most social interactions, so if you are going all out to leave your mark, chances are you'll either appear uptight or you'll end up dominating the situation and coming across as pushy.

RELAX

Have you ever noticed how the people who tend to impress us the most are the ones who don't seek our approval? We all admire people who are comfortable in their own skin, and don't have to try too hard. So relax and stop wasting all of your mental and physical resources on trying to impress other people.

DRESS FOR SUCCESS

Just because you aren't falling over yourself to impress doesn't mean you shouldn't be dressed and groomed to make the absolute best of yourself. Sloppy style impresses no one. If you are afraid that dressing smart will make you look square, consider the alternative: dressing badly will only make you look like a loser (rather than someone who is too cool to care about their appearance). Take a moment to analyze the physical image you present to the world. List five ways in which it can be improved, and take action now.

> "Sometimes one creates a dynamic impression by saying something, and sometimes one creates as significant an impression by remaining silent."
>
> —*Dalai Lama, spiritual leader*
>
> "If you want to win friends, make it a point to remember them. If you remember my name, you pay me a subtle compliment; you indicate that I have made an impression on you. Remember my name and you add to my feeling of importance."
>
> —*Dale Carnegie, motivational speaker and author*

WISE MEN SAY

LEARN HOW TO SHAKE HANDS

Introduce yourself with a smile and a firm handshake (this lies somewhere between limp and bone-crushing; practice on a friend if you haven't yet discovered this happy medium).

LISTEN AND OBSERVE

First, listen to people's names during an introduction and remember them. Then evaluate the scene. You won't have the first clue of how to join a conversation and make an appropriate contribution unless you are able to judge the mood and the focus of the other people in the room. In order to function in any environment you need to understand its dynamics, which means spending some time listening and observing.

MIND YOUR MANNERS

People might not notice your politeness, but they will certainly take note of inappropriate behavior. Be punctual, follow rules and regulations, and don't do anything you wouldn't do in a job interview. Don't get too familiar too soon. It's much better to leave people wanting more than to give them your life story in the first ten minutes.

BE A GIVER, NOT A TAKER

We all need stuff from other people in order to get ahead in life, and nowhere is this more apparent than in business. Pushy salespeople fail every time because they don't succeed in convincing other people that they have something good to offer; instead, they leave the impression that they want to take something, usually your money. It's the same with social interactions, both professional and personal. So be a giver, not a taker. Four ways to do this include the following:

1. Listen more than you talk.

2. Show interest in other people and ask for nothing in return.

3. Be positive and enthusiastic.

4. Above all, make people feel important.

WIN AN ARM WRESTLE

A rm wrestling is a test of strength, but it is also a sport in which technique and knowledge of the power of leverage can greatly affect the outcome, even between opponents of differing strength. The techniques below will be sure to give you a winning edge.

PUT YOUR BEST FOOT FORWARD

Most amateur arm wrestlers completely overlook the importance of their stance. If you are wrestling with your right arm, sit with your right foot farther forward than your left; if you are using your left arm, place your left foot farther forward than your right. This stance gives you optimum leverage and makes it easier for you to keep your arm as close to your body as possible.

THE GRIP

When you grip your opponent's hand, place your index finger over your thumb. This is called wrapping, and is an important component of the "toproll" (see below).

ARM POSITION

Keep your arm as close to your body as possible, so you will be able to use your whole body as leverage as well as maximize the strength in your upper body, especially your shoulders. If you allow your opponent to pull your arm away from your body, you will be forced to rely on forearm strength and will lose a lot of leverage.

MAKE AN EXPLOSIVE START

Many arm wrestles are won or lost in the first second. Keep your arm and fist inside your shoulders, then try to gain control of your opponent's wrist using the "hook" or "toproll" technique.

APPLY SIDE AND BACK PRESSURE

Most people exert only side pressure, as they attempt to press their opponent's arm sideways. You should also exert back pressure, however, driving your fist toward your own body. When you pull your opponent's arm away from his body and toward your shoulder, not only do you weaken his leverage but you also increase your own.

"Strength is magical; just a little bit more can mean the difference between success and failure."

—*Mike Berry, athletic trainer and coach*

"Spirit has fifty times the strength and staying power of brawn and muscle."

—*Mark Twain, author and satirist*

WISE MEN SAY

WINNING TECHNIQUES

Catch your opponent off guard with these pro arm-wrestling moves:

THE HOOK Snap your wrist toward you with an explosive burst in the first split second of the contest. If successful, you will gain greater leverage because your hand will be higher than your opponent's.

THE TOPROLL Try to walk your fingers up your opponent's hand to gain maximum leverage while applying continuous, maximum back pressure. This will give you a leverage advantage from which you can press on to victory.

THE PRESS If your chest and triceps strength is superior to that of your opponent, maneuver his palm until it is face-up to the ceiling, with your hand on top. From this position you can perform the press. Get your body over your arm and press down using your upper body and arm.

DEVELOP YOUR WRISTS AND FOREARMS

In arm wrestling, leverage and technique are greatly enhanced by brute strength. These two exercises will give you forearms and wrists of steel.

SLEDGEHAMMER RAISES Grip a sledgehammer by its handle and place the head on the floor in front of you. Keeping your arm by your side, raise the head so that the shaft is parallel to the ground by pivoting your wrist, rather than moving your arm. Repeat to failure. Then repeat the exercise, only this time with the head behind you.

POWER WRIST CURLS Place weights on a short barbell and grip either end. In a sitting position, and starting with your wrists in line with your forearms, curl your wrists toward you to their full contraction, then return to the starting position, keeping control of the weight at all times. Repeat to failure.

COMPLAIN AND GET RESULTS

Sometimes a guy has to stand up for his rights. What do you do when things haven't gone according to plan, and you want to complain? Perhaps you want to return faulty goods, a service has been unsatisfactory, or you've been kept waiting or received poor customer care.

You might seek financial compensation, a replacement item, or merely an apology. If you kick up a fuss, lose your temper, and make life difficult for everyone, you might get what you want, but you may also alienate those who are trying to resolve your problem. The best strategy is to smile, stay calm and polite, explain the problem clearly and briefly, and make allies, not enemies. The following ten tips will guide you to the goal of 100 percent satisfaction:

1. Start the conversation with the assumption that the other person wants to resolve your problem (which is usually true—most of us like to please). Right away you will feel more positive and cooperative and less antagonistic.

2. Make sure that you are talking to a person who has the time and, most importantly, the authority to help you. When in doubt, ask to speak to a manager or someone in authority. In general, the higher up you go, the better your chances of a favorable and speedy result. Many complaints are resolved swiftly as soon as they have been brought to the attention of senior management.

3. Always get the name of the person you are talking to, especially when you are on the phone. Keep a record of the time and duration of each call and what was discussed or agreed to.

4. Make it clear that you do not blame the other person for the problem. It is your job to get them on your side so they will be more inclined to help you.

5. Explain your situation calmly and quietly. Keep your body language open and relaxed in person, and talk rationally and politely on the phone.

6. Try to talk about the matter objectively, rather than becoming emotional. You need the other person to fix your problem, not change your mood. Getting emotional or threatening will usually cause the other person to feel blamed and defensive.

7. Smile. Who would you think is more assertive—a person who states what they want while smiling, or frowning? You can smile and still mean business. People will respond more favorably to your smile, because it shows that you are not a physical threat.

8. Once you've got someone to listen to your complaint, make sure you thank them for taking the time and effort to help you, and make it clear what result you are expecting.

9. End the conversation with a question that invites empathy with your situation. For example, say something like, "I'm not being unreasonable, am I?" or "I'm sure you can understand why I am feeling upset?" and "You'd do the same thing in my position, right?" It is difficult for an employee to answer "No" to direct questions such as these without sounding unhelpful. It's a subtle way to enlist them into your service! A smile or nod as you say it will reinforce it even further.

10. Whatever the outcome, thank the person for their time. If you didn't get a resolution, ask for the name and contact details of someone with more authority. Make sure you get the name of the person who originally helped you, so that you make it clear that you mean business. Remember, tenacity is the better part of valor.

"To say nothing, especially when speaking, is half the art of diplomacy."

—*Will Durant, Pulitzer Prize-winning author and philosopher*

"If you have time to whine and complain about something, then you have the time to do something about it."

—*Anthony J. D'Angelo, motivational speaker and author*

WISE MEN SAY

THE ART OF ARCHERY

While it takes skill and, of course, artistry to handle a bow and arrow, the advice below will help to guide you on your way to mastering this most ancient of weapons.

TEST FOR EYE DOMINANCE

Before you pick up a bow and let loose your first arrow, you'll need to discover which of your eyes is dominant, because this is what determines in which hand you should hold the bow. Pick an object far away, and with both eyes open point at it with your index finger. Now close each eye in turn. When your dominant eye is closed, your finger will appear to move away from the image. When your other eye is closed, your finger should appear to stay over the object.

If your left eye is dominant, you should hold the bow in your right hand; if your right eye is dominant, hold the bow in your left hand. If you are left-handed and left-eye dominant or right-handed and right-eye dominant, however, it is probably better to favor your hand (and arm strength for pulling back the bowstring), rather than your dominant eye.

STANCE

Stand facing the target with your feet about shoulder width apart. Imagine a line running from between your legs to the bulls-eye on the target. This is your shooting line. Your weight should be evenly balanced on both feet and between heel and foot. Keep your feet in this position, and maintain this balance while you aim and shoot.

NOCK THE ARROW

Place the shaft of the arrow on the arrow rest, and nock the arrow by placing the nock (the plastic V-groove on the back of the arrow) onto the bowstring just above your index finger (this will be marked by a colored nocking-point locator). Make sure that the "index fletch" (also known as the cock feather) on the arrow is pointing away from the bow.

Place the arrow nock between but not touching your index and middle fingers, then curl your first three fingers in line around the bowstring (so that the string rests in the first joints). Keep the back of your hand as flat and relaxed as possible, bend your pinkie out of the way, and tuck your thumb into your palm. Pull on the bowstring slightly, ready for the "draw."

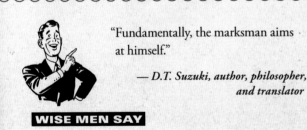

"Fundamentally, the marksman aims at himself."

— *D.T. Suzuki, author, philosopher, and translator*

WISE MEN SAY

DRAW

Place your outstretched palm on the handle of the bow, and position it so that the centerline of the V is in the middle of your thumb and index finger. Now grip the handle, but keep your fingers and thumb relaxed (the pressure of the draw goes through the thumb muscle).

Lift your head and look at the target. Push your bow arm out while raising both arms, keeping your front shoulder in its normal position, and raise the elbow of your drawing arm above your hand, so that you engage your back muscles for the draw.

Now, without moving your head or body, push your bow hand forward and pull the elbow of your drawing arm backward until your index finger is against your jaw, your thumb is against your neck, and the bowstring is against your chin and nose.

AIM

Maintain bow tension as you move the bow so that the sight pin is lined up with the bulls-eye. The bowstring and the edge of the bow should be parallel (if not, you have tilted the bow away from vertical).

FIRE

Release the arrow by relaxing all three bowstring fingers at once so that the string slides off them at the same time, as your hand continues to move backward and comes to a rest. Maintain this arm position (the follow-through) until the arrow has hit the target. Don't be tempted to move your head to see where the arrow has gone, until it has hit the target.

REST

Archery puts a lot of stress on the upper body, so it is vital that you pause between each shot for at least thirty seconds to give your muscles a rest.

PLAY CHESS

Can't tell your king from your rook? Always forget which piece moves in an L-shape? If your chess skills are a little rusty—or if you're new to the game—you'll find the basic rules and strategies of this ancient game here.

BASIC RULES

Chess is a game of skill and strategy for two players played on a checkered board of sixty-four alternating black and white squares. Each player starts the game with an "army" of sixteen pieces.

No two pieces may occupy the same square together. A player can capture an opponent's piece (apart from the king) by moving his piece into its square; the captured piece is then removed from the board and plays no further part in the game (but see below for "promoting" a pawn).

The king cannot be taken, but it can be put in "check" when it is threatened by another piece (i.e., if the other piece could legally move into the square occupied by the king). If this happens, the other player must immediately move his king out of check, move another piece to block the check, or capture the attacking piece. If the player is unable to get out of check, "checkmate" is declared and he loses the game. At the start of the game the pieces are set up as follows:

Note that there should be a white square at the bottom right-hand corner of each player's side of the board. White always makes the first move, then players take turns.

Once a player touches a piece they must move it (unless by doing so they would perform an illegal move).

THE PIECES

Each player begins the game with eight pawns, two knights, two bishops, two rooks, one queen, and one king. The king is the most important piece (if your king goes down, you lose), but the queen is the most powerful, followed by the rook, the bishop, the knight, and the pawn.

PAWN The pawns are the foot soldiers. Individually they are the least valuable pieces, but together they can be used tactically to dominate the game. They can move forward only one square at a time, or one or two squares on their first move. They threaten the two squares diagonally in front of them. If a pawn reaches the other side of the board it can be turned into any other piece (usually a queen), apart from a king.

BISHOP The bishop threatens other pieces by moving in straight lines diagonally up and down the board, but it cannot jump over other pieces. One bishop remains on the white squares throughout the game while the other moves on the black squares.

ROOK Also known as the castle, the rook threatens other pieces by moving in straight lines horizontally or vertically, but it cannot jump over other pieces.

KNIGHT The knight threatens other pieces by moving in an L-shape, and it is the only piece that can jump over other pieces. It moves one or two squares horizontally or vertically followed by two or one square perpendicular to the others.

QUEEN The most powerful piece on the board, the queen threatens other pieces by moving diagonally, horizontally, or vertically, but it cannot jump over other pieces.

KING The king moves one square at a time in any direction, provided it does not move into "check." The king can also capture opposing pieces on adjacent squares.

SPECIAL MOVES

CASTLING The king and a rook can perform this move as long as neither piece has yet moved; there are no other pieces between the rook and the king; the king is not in check; and the king would not pass through check or end up in check after the move. To castle, move the king two spaces toward the rook, then move the rook next to the king on the inside.

EN PASSANT When a pawn has made a double move, and passes through a square that is threatened by an opposing pawn, on the next move the opposing pawn can capture the enemy pawn by moving into the threatened square.

DRAW There are five ways in which the game may end in a draw.

1. By agreement: neither player has enough remaining pieces to win the game

2. Stalemate: a player is not in check but is unable to make a legal move

3. The fifty-move rule: if during fifty consecutive moves no pieces are taken and no pawns have been moved, any player from then on may declare a draw at any time as long as no pawns are moved or pieces are taken

4. The three-times-move rule: the same board position is repeated three times in a row

5. Perpetual check: a player is able to check an opponent forever by alternating between two checking positions

BUILD A SHELTER IN THE WILD

Building a shelter in the wild is one of the skills that can make the difference between life and death. You can go a few days without food or water, but without proper shelter you'll be in real trouble fast.

LOCATION

This is the most important consideration when building a shelter. As survival expert Tom Brown says, "A good shelter in a bad location is a bad shelter." Stay away from clearings and large bodies of water, as these are most susceptible to the elements. Sheltering among trees is good, as long as you don't venture too far into the forest or scrub, where bugs, damp, and flooding hazards are greater. If possible, make for higher ground.

SIZE

The function of a shelter is to enable you to maintain normal body temperature. Therefore, make your shelter as small as possible. It will not only require less energy to build but will also allow you to regulate heat better.

LEAN-TO This is probably the easiest and quickest shelter to build. Site your shelter so that the opening faces away from the prevailing wind. Find a large branch or log and lean it against something solid (tree, boulder, etc.), such that the top end is three or four feet off the ground. Next lay smaller branches along the main pole, lash them at the top, and bury them into the ground at the bottom for added structural integrity. (Alternatively, make the frame by driving two Y-shaped sticks into the ground a few feet apart, then balance another branch on top of the "Y" to form a ridgepole, and lean branches against it.) Starting at the bottom and working upward, thatch and insulate the structure with large leaves, grass, bark, bracken, and sticks to keep out the wind, rain, and snow.

TEPEE The frame of this simple tepee is made by lashing the tops of three long branches together. Plant the thicker ends of the braches on the ground, so that the structure has a solid base. Then lean smaller branches and foliage around the tripod, and add even smaller sticks to fill in the gaps. Use lots of leaves and bark for insulation, and leave a small entrance.

SNOW CAVE If you are stranded in snow and have to wait to be rescued, you can dig a hole in the snow to provide protection from the wind. Choose a site free from the threat of avalanche, and make the entrance to the cave on the leeward side of a slope, where there will be more snow to work with (you'll need at least five feet of snow). Digging a snow cave will take a couple of hours and will use a lot of energy. Try to stay dry while you dig.

Dig a tunnel into the slope, about three feet in diameter and eight feet in length. Then start excavating upward and outward until you have dug a cave that you can sit up in. Create a smooth, arched chamber, so that melting snow will run down the sides rather than drip onto you. Make a sleeping platform shelf at the back of the cave. Make sure the entrance is lower than the floor, so that warm air does not escape. Create two ventilation holes by poking a ski pole (or any suitable stick) through the side of the ceiling. Keep the stick in the hole and waggle it periodically to keep the ventilation hole clear. Seal the entrance with empty backpacks. Cut niches in the walls and place some candles in them, if possible: this can raise the temperature significantly as well as provide light.

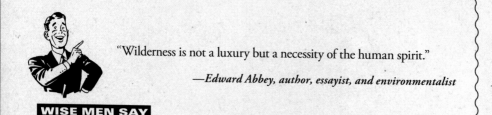

"Wilderness is not a luxury but a necessity of the human spirit."

—*Edward Abbey, author, essayist, and environmentalist*

WISE MEN SAY

WRITE A THANK-YOU NOTE

Do you have a shameful inability to write sincere and appropriate thank-you notes? If yes, then it's high time you did something about it. If nothing can motivate you to dig out a pen and paper and start writing, consider this: thank-you notes actually increase the frequency and value of the gifts you receive. Ready now?

Use a pen with blue ink and a good quality blank note card or sheets of stationery paper. If you don't already own these, invest in some. Don't use a sheet of printer paper, because you'll need to write only a few lines, and they will look meager surrounded by a sea of white. Avoid commercial thank-you cards; they are unnecessary, and it is your personal touch that is important. A store-bought card looks plain lazy.

BRAIN FOOD

What is the maximum number of times a normal sheet of paper can be folded in half by hand?

Solution: Once, because after that it is being folded into quarters, eighths, etc.

ANATOMY OF A THANK YOU

Every thank-you note should contain these six elements:

1. Say hello to the person you are thanking. It seems obvious, but you'd be surprised how many people forget to directly address the person they are thanking. Even the most heartfelt thank you will feel unfocused and impersonal if you don't greet the giver.

2. Say thank you in the first sentence. There's no need to fluff around with fillers like, "I just thought I'd drop you a quick note to say . . ." or "I am writing to you . . ." These are clumsy expressions that cloud the directness of your message.

Use the present tense, so that your gratitude sounds spontaneous and fresh. Don't say, "I loved the train set: I played with it all Christmas"; rather say, "I love the train set and have been playing with it all Christmas." It's a subtle difference but helps to lend immediacy to your feelings.

If someone has sent you cash, don't mention the amount. Instead of saying, "Thank you for the fifty bucks; it was very kind of you," be a bit more subtle and say something like, "Thank you for your generosity" or "your kindness."

If the giver has provided you with something other than a "thing" (letting you stay at their place, treating you to dinner, mentioning you favorably to a potential employer, etc.), then you should name the service they have provided, with an appropriate degree of vagueness. For example, you wouldn't want to say, "Thank you for helping me get that job," but you might say, "Thank you for taking the time and effort to talk with _____. I really appreciate it."

3. Write something positive about the item (or service) and how you intend to use it. For example, if someone has given you a pair of cufflinks, you might say, "I'm sure I'll get lots of admiring glances when I wear them at James's wedding next month." This shows not only that you like the cufflinks and are proud of them but also that you are prepared to wear them on such an important occasion. Or if you intend to wear them every day, you could write, "I've been wearing them every day at work." If the gift was cash, suggest how the money might come in handy, but spare them a blow-by-blow breakdown of how you intend to account for every cent.

4. Mention a future meeting. Show the giver that he or she is and will continue to be an important part of your life. Back to the cufflinks: "I hope to see you again soon at James's wedding. You can be sure I'll be wearing the cufflinks." Even if you both know that you probably won't see each other again for months, even years, you can still say something like, "You are in my thoughts" or "It seems so long since we have seen each other. I do hope our paths cross again sometime soon."

5. Say thank you again, just before you say goodbye. Nothing elaborate, just "Thanks again for your lovely gift." This sentence winds down the note and gives the reader advance warning that it is coming to an end.

6. Don't forget to include the appropriate closing—"With love," "Regards," "Yours truly," etc.—followed by your name.

"Silent gratitude isn't much use to anyone."

—*G.B. Stern, novelist*

"Make it a habit to tell people thank you. To express your appreciation, sincerely and without the expectation of anything in return. Truly appreciate those around you, and you'll soon find many others around you. Truly appreciate life, and you'll find that you have more of it."

—*Ralph Marston, motivational speaker and marketing consultant*

WISE MEN SAY

PERFORM THE HEIMLICH MANEUVER

Every year about 3,000 people die by inhaling or choking on food. When food gets stuck in the airway it obstructs breathing and can lead to oxygen starvation and permanent brain damage within minutes. If the Heimlich maneuver is performed decisively and correctly, however, it is often successful, which is why it is routinely taught in first aid courses. Here is a step-by-step guide to performing this procedure (but it is no substitute for proper first aid training):

- Before attempting the Heimlich maneuver, first ask the person if they are choking. If they can speak and/or breathe or are coughing forcefully, don't perform the maneuver. It is not only pointless but also dangerous to perform the Heimlich maneuver on someone who isn't actually choking, because it diverts attention away from the real cause of danger, whatever that might be. Apply several firm backslaps first. If this fails to remove the airway obstruction, use the Heimlich maneuver.

HEIMLICH HOW-TO

1. Stand behind the person and reach both of your arms around his or her waist. Make a fist with your dominant hand, with your thumb facing inward, toward the victim, just above the navel and below the rib cage.

2. Grab your fist tightly with your other hand, and pull upward and inward abruptly five times. This action should be quite hard, but not so much as to cause damage to ribs or internal organs. This will force air out of the lungs, dislodge the obstruction, and force it into the victim's mouth by generating a cough by artificial means.

3. Take extra care if the victim is elderly or a child, as they can be more easily injured. If the obstruction doesn't clear on the first attempt, thrust again. Keep a firm grip on the victim in case he or she loses consciousness and collapses.

4. If repeated attempts still fail to clear the airway, call emergency services immediately, as it may be necessary to perform a tracheotomy.

"President Bush got through the Super Bowl without event. The Secret Service pre-chewed his pretzels."

—*David Letterman, host of Emmy Award-winning talk show*

WISE MEN SAY

HAVE A HEALTHY HEART

Your heart is an amazing organ. During your lifetime it will pump a staggering 3 billion times. There is no such thing as a sudden heart attack; it takes years of preparation. It's never too late to start taking better care of your most precious organ, however, so be smart and have a healthy heart.

GET PLENTY OF EXERCISE

You should do a minimum of thirty minutes of moderate physical activity on most days of the week, but that doesn't mean that you have to go and sweat it out at the gym for hours on end. You can even break down your exercise into two fifteen-minute sessions, or three sessions of ten minutes. A half-hour brisk walk is a fantastic way to get the blood pumping, reduce your cholesterol and blood pressure, and burn some calories without putting too much stress on your joints. The best exercise is the one you feel good about and can do over and over again, as an enjoyable part of your daily routine.

DIET

Eat a low-fat diet that is high in fiber, fruit, and vegetables (at least five portions a day). That doesn't mean that you can't treat yourself, and you shouldn't have to cut any food out of your diet, as long as you are sensible for the majority of the time. Figure out which foods are your downfall and cut down on them (but don't stop eating them altogether).

You should get no more than 30 percent of your daily intake of calories from fat, and less than 10 percent of your total calories from saturated fats. Keep your sodium intake below 3,000 mg per day, and cut down on caffeine, MSG, and other food additives. For men, drinking a small glass of red wine every day has been found to be beneficial to the heart and to reduce the chances of a heart attack.

LOWER YOUR CHOLESTEROL

Cholesterol is a type of fat, which has good and bad effects on the body. When your body has too much cholesterol, fat deposits form on the inside of the blood vessel walls and can restrict blood flow, so that the heart has to work much harder to pump blood around the body. If the vessels become blocked, this can lead to a heart attack or stroke.

Exercising regularly and watching what you eat will lower your cholesterol. Limit the amount of butter and margarine you eat and avoid hydrogenated oils. Choose low-fat dairy options and eat fish and chicken more often than red meat. Reduce the amount of fried food you eat, trim all visible fat from your meat, and avoid fatty desserts.

LOWER YOUR BLOOD PRESSURE

A blood pressure level of 140 over 90 mm Hg (millimeters of mercury) or higher is considered high. About 50 million American adults have high blood pressure, also called hypertension. High blood pressure makes the heart work extra hard and hardens artery walls, increasing the risk of heart disease and stroke. Reducing alcohol consumption, performing regular exercise, and losing excess weight lowers your blood pressure.

"You can survive a stroke, but the high prices for medication can give you a heart attack."

—*Bernie Mac, stand-up comedian and actor*

"Except for an occasional heart attack I feel as young as I ever did."

—*Robert Benchley, humorist and actor*

WISE MEN SAY

QUIT SMOKING

The carbon monoxide in cigarette smoke reduces the blood's ability to carry oxygen and makes the heart beat faster. Smoking increases cholesterol levels as well as levels of a blood-clotting protein called fibrinogen, so that the blood becomes stickier. Smokers have twice the risk of having a heart attack than do non-smokers. Whatever a person's age, it is never too late to give up smoking. In the first year after you quit smoking this risk drops dramatically, and levels will gradually return to normal.

BRAIN FOOD

If there are six apples on a table and you take away four, how many do you have?

Solution: You have four.

MINIMIZE STRESS

It is well known that a major cause of stress is working too hard and not taking enough time to do the things that are enjoyable and relaxing. Additionally consider, however, that the underlying cause of stress may also be one of the following: low self-esteem, procrastination, feelings of too much responsibility, fear of failure, trying to be perfect, guilt, grief, suppressed anger, and depression.

Make a list of what needs to be done and prioritize, because keeping all of your tasks in your head is very stressful in and of itself. Perform only one task at a time and give it all of your concentration, rather than worrying about everything else that needs to be done. Spend most of your time on the most important tasks; don't waste time on trivia. Delegate and ask for help. Give yourself plenty of rewards for getting things done. Take plenty of short breaks. Above all, count your blessings every morning and maintain a sense of perspective throughout the day.

GET BIGGER BICEPS

There's nothing more impressive than a set of killer arms, but many guys fail to see the growth they want, despite spending hours at the gym. Take your biceps to new heights (literally!) with these simple training tips.

GET PLENTY OF REST

Overtraining is one of the biggest reasons for disappointing muscle growth. If you want your biceps to get bigger, then you need to give them time to rest, because muscles grow only when they are at rest, not while you are working out. The biceps are one of the easiest muscles to overtrain because they are involved in so many upper-body exercises. So, perform only one biceps-targeted muscle workout per week, and your biceps will still get plenty of activity during your other workouts. Rest at least twenty-four hours between heavy-weights sessions.

DECREASE THE WEIGHTS AND INCREASE THE REPS

Range of motion is more important than the size of the weights that you lug around to impress other gym users. Increase your range of motion; exercising over the full range of the muscle's motion is the only way to target all of the fibers and achieve maximum growth. When you are doing biceps curls, start each one at full "pronation" (arm extended) and finish at full "supination" (arm curled, pinky turned in toward body). If you can't do this you are using too much weight, so reduce the weight until you can.

"Biceps," in Latin, means "two heads."

SQUEEZE AT THE TOP OF THE CURL

When you reach the top of a bicep curl, squeeze the bicep for a couple of seconds to create an even more intense pump. This will encourage the muscle cells to thicken and will spur the growth of new muscle fibers.

SOME BICEPS-TARGETING EXERCISES

STANDING BARBELL CURL Standing with your feet shoulder width apart, hold the barbell with your hands a little less than shoulder width apart. Start with your arms lowered so that the bar almost rests on your thighs (don't lock out completely or you'll overstress your joints). Lift the bar until your biceps are fully contracted, while keeping your back straight. Only use weights that you can lift in a controlled motion. If you have to grab forcefully, or heave with your back, the weight is too heavy. Lower the bar in a controlled motion. Do two sets of twelve reps. Rest for two minutes, then increase the weight and do another eight reps with your hands six inches apart.

SEATED BARBELL CURL Sit on a bench and rest a barbell on your lap. Grip the bar with both hands at shoulder width, with your knuckles pointing toward the floor. Curl upward to your chin, then back again, controlling the weight all the way; do eight reps. Seated curls allow you to lift more weight than standing curls do. Use the maximum weight you can handle without losing form.

SEATED DUMBBELL CURL Sit on a bench with your legs spread while holding a dumbbell in your hand. Rest your right elbow against your inner thigh, just behind your knee. Curl the dumbbell up until it won't go any farther, while keeping your elbow on your thigh, then lower slowly. Do three sets of ten reps with each arm.

"There are some girls that are turned on by my body, and some others who are turned off. But for the majority I just use it as a conversation piece. Like someone walking a cheetah down 42nd Street would have a natural conversation piece. Then when they get to talking to me they see I am not mean but gentle to them, and that's all they want to know."

—Arnold Schwarzenegger, professional body builder, actor, and U.S. governor

WISE MEN SAY

PADDLE A CANOE

It looks easy, but paddling a canoe correctly is a skill that can take years to master. Here, we've summarized the basics for you. (Remember: always wear a life jacket in a canoe, and cover up and wear sunscreen if you are in strong sunlight, as the sun's rays will reflect off the water and burn you more quickly than they would on land.)

NINE PADDLING TECHNIQUES

1. Sit or kneel in the canoe facing forward, either at the stern or the bow if there are two of you, or in the middle if you are alone. Kneeling offers greater stability, as your center of gravity is lower. If there are two of you, paddle on opposite sides of the canoe.

2. Hold the top of the paddle's handle with your inside hand, and with the other hand grip the paddle two or three feet down the shaft, with your knuckles pointing outward.

3. Place the blade of the paddle in the water—at least three feet in front of you—reaching with your lower hand as far out as possible without lunging forward.

4. Think of each stroke as moving the canoe forward, toward the paddle. Push your top hand forward and your bottom hand back to draw the blade smoothly through the water, keeping the handle perpendicular to the water (don't bring the paddle across your body as you would in a rowboat, as this will make the canoe turn). Keep the top of the handle just below eye level.

5. Pivot your shoulder so that the paddle blade comes straight back, rather than follows the shape of the canoe.

6. At the end of the stroke the blade should be level with your hip. If you bring the paddle back any farther, you will actually slow the canoe down and waste energy as well as put too much strain on your back.

7. After each stroke, quickly lift the blade out of the water and turn the paddle so that the blade is parallel to the water as you bring it forward, ready for the next stroke.

"Travel a thousand miles by train and you are a brute; pedal five hundred on a bicycle and you remain basically a bourgeois; paddle a hundred in a canoe and you are already a child of nature."

—Pierre Elliott Trudeau, former Canadian prime minister

"Everyone must believe in something. I believe I'll go canoeing."

—Henry David Thoreau, author, naturalist, and philosopher

"A true Canadian is one who can make love in a canoe without tipping."

—Pierre Berton, author, journalist, and television personality

WISE MEN SAY

8. Don't paddle too vigorously. A slow stroke, followed by a glide before the next stroke, is much more sustainable over long distances and conserves energy. You can also switch sides every five or six strokes to give your arms a change. When paddling in pairs, one canoeist calls "hut" to indicate a change of side.

9. If the canoe veers off course, bring it back into line by performing a "J-stroke." Flip the paddle out at the end of a forward stroke and either "pry" (push out) or "rudder" (use the paddle as such) to keep going in a straight line.

AVOID JET LAG

It is impossible to travel halfway round the world in an airplane and not suffer a little bit from jet lag, but there are several precautions you can take to help your body and its internal clock cope with the time difference, so you'll arrive at your destination feeling refreshed and ready to be your charming self.

PLAN AHEAD

The better prepared you are pre-flight, the less stress you will place on your mind and body. If you remain calm and organized, your trip will be more manageable. Before the flight get lots of sleep, eat healthily, avoid drinking alcohol, and get plenty of exercise. If you are stressed out before the flight, this stress will only increase during and after your journey. Adjust your sleeping habits by an hour each night for a few days before you travel, to prepare your body for the new time zone.

FLY WEST

There is some evidence to suggest that flying westward causes less disruption than flying eastward.

RESET YOUR WATCH

At the beginning of your flight, set your watch to the local time of your destination, and sleep or stay awake accordingly. If you arrive at your destination during daytime, stay awake until evening. Go out into the sunshine, which will send powerful daytime signals to your body clock. If you succumb to sleep during the day you are telling your body clock that you are still at home.

DRINK LOTS OF FLUIDS

The pressurized atmosphere in an airplane is very dehydrating, so it is vital that you drink plenty of water. Avoid sugary juices as well as sodas, alcohol, and caffeinated beverages. Alcohol not only dehydrates, its intoxicating effects are also exaggerated under pressurized conditions.

STAY ACTIVE

Get up frequently, move around, and do stretching exercises to allow the blood to circulate around your body and to help reduce the risk of deep vein thrombosis. Even while seated you should twist your ankles around and flex your wrists from time to time.

PAMPER YOURSELF

Those neck pillows, sleeping masks, and earplugs that are on sale in airports will actually help you to get a better night's sleep. Take off your shoes before you sleep, as your feet will swell, and don't use sleeping tablets, as they have a dehydrating effect and will cause you to lie knocked out in the same position for several hours, which is bad for your muscles and circulation.

THE ANTI-JET-LAG DIET

It isn't just your sleeping patterns that are disrupted by being in a different time zone; your digestive system also has to adjust to meals during what used to be the middle of the night for you. So go easy on your stomach for the first few days after traveling, and eat small portions with plenty of fresh fruit and vegetables. Avoid fatty foods, which are harder to digest, even though you may crave them when you're tired. Eat high-protein foods if you want to stay awake and high-carb foods if you want to encourage sleep.

BUY A SPEEDBOAT

I f you're flush with cash and you've got plenty of it to splash around, why not buy the definitive boy toy, a speedboat? Not only is it the ultimate status symbol, messing about in your boat is great fun, too. So here are a few tips on how to get more boat for your buck:

WHAT'S THE POINT?

No, really—what do you want to use your speedboat for? Are you planning on impressing your business contacts by taking them on cocktail-filled mini-jaunts, or is your boat going to be more of a floating bachelor pad, the ideal place to romance a succession of special ladies? If entertaining is your thing, make sure the galley (that's sea-speak for the kitchen) is up to the job, and don't skimp on the cabin arrangements.

Also consider whether you will use the boat on the open seas or on a lake or river. There's little point in going for high-spec oceangoing capabilities if you plan to hug the coast or cruise the lake. This will determine the size, speed, and stability of the boat you buy as well as factors such as the length, beam (width), and draft (depth of the boat beneath the water). Don't buy a monster-size craft if you will need to negotiate narrow stretches of water frequently, but bear in mind that a smaller boat is less safe in open water. Also, watch out for fuel consumption; some boats get only a handful of miles to the gallon when the throttle is wide open.

Hull design and angle make an important contribution to the amount of available cabin space. Single hulls are the most spacious, whereas twin-hull catamarans offer greater stability but are more cramped.

WHO MAKES THE BEST BOATS?

As with cars, in the end it comes down to personal choice, but there are lots of top boat brands to choose from, including Cigarette, Cobra, Donzi, Formula, Fountain, and Mares. You can get a simple thirty-footer for about the same price as a small family home, but the upper limit depends on your tastes and the size of your wallet. For example, the XSR48 combines the DNA and high performance of a supercar with super-yacht detailing to create the world's first true superboat, with a top speed of 110 miles per hour (96 knots), but you won't get much change out of $2 million, and only 100 will be made, so if you're not already on the waiting list, drool on.

SHOULD I BUY A HORSE INSTEAD?

Every week you should wash and dry the boat and inspect the moorings, knots, and fenders, as well as the hull fittings, engine (especially oil level), and electrics, otherwise your safety and insurance will be severely compromised. You'll also have to pay for moorings and over-winter storage.

"Who is staring at the sea is already sailing a little."

—*Paul Carvel, author and editor*

"If you want to build a ship, don't drum up people to collect wood and don't assign them tasks and work, but rather teach them to long for the endless immensity of the sea."

—*Antoine de Saint-Exupéry, author and aviator*

WISE MEN SAY

CHOP DOWN A TREE

If a tree falls in the woods and nobody's around to hear it, does it make a sound? We have no idea. We do, however, know the proper way to make a tree fall. So pick up that ax and discover your inner Paul Bunyan.

TREE-FELLING TIPS

Before you begin, sharpen your ax so that it is sharp enough to whittle wood, and check the handle for cracks. If you are using a chainsaw, check the oil and ensure that the chain is at the correct tension.

- Inspect the area surrounding the tree that you are going to fell and decide where you would like it to fall. Check wind direction, determine which way the tree is naturally weighted, and make sure the fall zone is free of people and obstacles, including power lines. Remove any vegetation or obstacles that obstruct your access to the tree. Do not fell a tree into the wind.

- Plan an escape route, so that if the tree falls in the wrong direction you can run to safety. Do not stand or walk behind the tree when it is falling, as it could kick back when it hits the ground. When the tree begins to fall, lay down your tool (or switch off the engine) and walk away at a 45-degree angle to the line of fall.

- Cut a notch a third of the way into the trunk, on the side of the tree to which you want it to fall. The bottom of the notch should be horizontal and the top sloping at a 45-degree angle. If the ax keeps getting stuck in the notch, cut another notch above it and then split the piece in between to widen it.

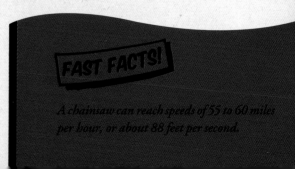

FAST FACTS!

A chainsaw can reach speeds of 55 to 60 miles per hour, or about 88 feet per second.

- Now make another notch on the opposite side of the tree in the same way, but two inches above the first one, and leave a section of wood in the middle of the tree (about $^{1}/_{6}$ of the diameter) that will act as a hinge when the tree falls, to prevent kickback.

- If the tree won't fall after you have cut the two notches, you should drive wedges into the second notch with a sledgehammer.

CHAINSAW SAFETY TIPS

Working with a chainsaw is no joke; there are about 30,000 chainsaw injuries each year. Here are five ways to stay safe:

1. Always start the chainsaw on the ground or on a stable surface, and use both hands.

2. The greatest danger when using a chainsaw is kickback, which accounts for one in five chainsaw injuries. When the tip of the saw comes into contact with something solid, such as a rock, log, or branch, the chainsaw kicks upward and can easily cause injury. For this reason, never saw with the tip of the blade.

3. Don't wear loose clothing or jewelry that could get caught up in the saw, and tie back long hair.

4. Don't use a chainsaw when you are feeling tired or under the weather. You need to maintain peak levels of concentration at all times.

5. Don't make cuts with the saw resting between your legs; cut with the saw outside your legs.

> "If trees could scream, would we be so cavalier about cutting them down? We might, if they screamed all the time, for no good reason."
>
> —*Jack Handey, humorist and television producer*

> "If I had eight hours to chop down a tree, I'd spend six hours sharpening my ax."
>
> —*Abraham Lincoln, former U.S. president*

WISE MEN SAY

CREATE THE ULTIMATE BACHELOR PAD

You may consider your living quarters just a place to crash after a hard day's work and a hard evening's play, but if you want a home that combines style and comfort, makes a statement about you, and is ready for anything, your pad may be in need of a makeover. You never know when that perfect woman will walk into your life and ask you to take her home. Plus, you need a comfortable place to kick back with the guys and watch the game. The overall design will be up to your individual tastes, but here are eight tips for transforming your ho-hum digs into a home that you can both live in and live up to:

1. Achieve a balance between style and coziness. Don't get too fixated on minimalist design at the expense of your day-to-day comfort and relaxation. The decor should be an expression and extension of your personality, so don't try to create an image that you can't live up to. A scheme that is an honest expression of your tastes will be much more welcoming than whatever image you think you should be projecting.

2. Leather sofas and chairs always look great in a bachelor pad, but make sure to try them out before you buy. Some are impossible to sit on, because your legs keep sliding off. Don't buy a cheap leather sofa, because it will look cheap. If your budget won't stretch to a leather sofa, get some leather accessories like cushions or an ottoman, or consider getting a slipcover (try ultrasuede), which is an inexpensive way to transform a tired old sofa into something your guests might actually want to sit on.

3. Buy plants only if you can be bothered to keep them in good condition. Sad, browning foliage won't help the ambience. If you are prepared to give them a little TLC, however, plants clean up the air in your living space, and they add color, life, and atmosphere.

4. Changing your lighting is an inexpensive way to smarten up your habitat. Consider using up-lights, downlights, spotlights, and those reliable and low-cost romantic standbys: candles.

5. Sort out your storage: it maximizes space and minimizes clutter. Find a place for everything and keep everything in its place (this is especially important in the bathroom). It looks better, and will help you to keep a clutter-free mind, so that you can concentrate on saving for that $9,000 flat-screen TV.

6. If you have a fireplace and a working chimney, you probably still can't be bothered to light a real fire very often. A simple and stylish modern gas or electric real-fire-effect model, however, is easy to install, cleaner than a real fire, and makes a great focal point.

7. No bachelor pad would be complete without a fully stocked bar. But there's no need to buy a high-end piece of furniture complete with bar stools. A less expensive solution—and one that takes up much less space than a proper bar—is to look for a metal or wooden cart on wheels that can be pushed out of the way during those rare times when the bar is not needed. Stylish art deco or midcentury modern examples can be found at yard sales, in thrift stores, or on eBay.

8. Remember, you don't have to create something totally new to transform an environment. Sometimes it can be better to work with what you've already got. Be brave and prepared to experiment but don't try too hard: the end result should look effortless.

CARVE A PUMPKIN

A pumpkin carved into a jack-o-lantern is the most familiar symbol of Halloween. Pumpkin-carving at the end of October is a centuries-old tradition, said to provide protection against evil spirits. If you haven't carved a pumpkin since you were a kid, here's how to do it properly:

TOOLS

To carve a good lantern you've got to have the right tools, most of which will probably already be in your kitchen drawers, or else you can buy a carving kit from any place that sells Halloween stuff.

LONG, THIN BONING KNIFE Use this for cutting the top hole and large pieces out of the face.

SMALL PARING KNIFE Use this for carving fine details. For this purpose a smaller knife is easier and safer to maneuver than a larger one.

CUTTING SAW This is useful for carving details, especially if the skin is tough.

STENCIL You can make a carving stencil by hand or on your computer, or download readymade ones from the Internet. Simply attach to the "front" of your pumpkin and prick along the lines with something sharp.

SPOONS Use a variety of spoons of various sizes to scoop out the flesh and seeds.

CHOOSE YOUR PUMPKIN

Choose a pumpkin that is big enough for your stencil; large ones are best for highly detailed work. Look for one that is free from marks, dents, or soft rotting patches. Place it on a flat surface and check for stability: a flat bottom will prevent it from rolling away.

CREATE THE LID

Use a long, thin boning knife to cut off a lid around the stem. Cut at an angle, so that when you replace the lid it won't fall inside the pumpkin. Make a hole a little wider than your fist, to give you enough room to scoop out the innards.

REMOVE THE SEEDS

Remove the seeds and the very soft flesh with your hands, then scrape the rest out with a spoon. Leave about one inch of flesh behind the face. Try to maintain a uniform thickness, otherwise you will weaken the structure and encourage premature rotting.

TRANSFER THE STENCIL

Tape your stencil to the pumpkin, making sure that the paper fits flatly around its contours then prick along the lines, spacing your holes closer together for areas of fine detail. Remove the stencil; if you have trouble seeing which bits to leave in and which to remove, use a black pen to shade in the bits that you want to end up as "holes."

"I would rather sit on a pumpkin, and have it all to myself, than be crowded on a velvet cushion."

—*Henry David Thoreau, author, naturalist, and philosopher*

WISE MEN SAY

CARVING

Place the pumpkin on a flat surface, or support it on your lap. Using a paring knife, carve the small details first, sawing along the dots. Work your way out from the center of the pumpkin, and carve the largest areas last, because once you have removed the large pieces the skin will become floppier and harder to carve. Don't twist the saw or knife, as it could break; for sharp turns, remove the tool and reinsert it at the correct angle. Keep all the pieces in place until the end, then remove them one by one, like a reverse jigsaw; that way you maintain structural support until the last moment. After carving, shine a flashlight into the pumpkin to view the details, and make last-minute adjustments where necessary. If any part of the design falls off, carefully reattach it with toothpicks.

KEEP IT FRESH

Rub petroleum jelly onto the inside of your jack-o-lantern and along the cut edges; this helps to retain moisture and slows down the dehydration process. Keep the pumpkin in the fridge or submerged in water until it is ready to use. You can even buy a spray-on preserver to protect against mold and bugs.

HOST A BARBECUE

When the sun is baking hot and the beer is nice and cold, the last thing you want to be doing is slaving over a hot stove; a barbecue, however, is a different ballgame altogether. It's fun and easy, and you won't miss out on the party atmosphere as long as you make a few preparations in advance.

INVITATIONS

Summer weekends are precious and few—and they book up fast. So whether you're sending paper invitations, e-mail invites, or asking people in person, if you're planning to host a big crowd it's best to invite people at least a week in advance, so they can plan their schedules accordingly. Your invitation should let them know when to arrive and when they can expect to start eating. That way they won't starve to death while waiting for you to burn the sausages. If there are families with small kids coming, plan to start doling out grub by early evening at the latest.

WHAT TO SERVE

Meat usually takes center stage at any barbecue, and there's nothing better than a perfectly grilled hamburger with all the fixings. But don't forget that many veggies can be thrown on the grill, too. Peppers, onions, and corn on the cob as well as many other veggies grill up beautifully, and are terrific accompaniments to the main course. If you're bored with burgers and dogs, try a theme such as Mexican, Caribbean, Hawaiian, or Moroccan. Whatever you decide to serve, always follow the golden rule of barbecues: make sure the meat is cooked properly. If it burns on the outside, chances are it will be undercooked on the inside.

PREPARE THE DAY BEFORE

The great thing about barbecues is that most of the food can be prepared in advance, including dips and a range of other appetizers. If you're making kebabs, cut up the meat and leave it to marinate in the fridge overnight. If you make your own burgers, you'll need to refrigerate them for a few hours before grilling to firm them up. Hot dogs and veggie burgers come ready to cook. It's really only the seafood, such as shrimp, that you will need to buy fresh on the same day. It's also best to wait until the day of the party to make salads or cut up vegetables like onions and peppers, otherwise they will become limp.

SIDES AND MUNCHIES

If you are following a theme it should give you lots of ideas for sides and munchies. A Mexican theme, for example, cries out for chips with salsa and guacamole, while a Moroccan theme suggests pita chips with hummus and baba ghanoush. Supply your guests with plenty of snacks—chips, olives, nuts, etc.—to nibble on while you're working your magic with the grill.

DRINKS

Buy a new plastic or metal bin from a hardware store and fill it full of ice and water to keep your beer and wine cool. Encourage your guests to help themselves to drinks; you want people to feel that they don't have to wait for a refill. Make up some pitchers of Sangria, Margaritas, or a themed cocktail—Mai Tais, anyone?—and your guests will love you. But don't forget to have plenty of soft drink options available, too, as well as jugs of ice water.

KNOW YOUR EQUIPMENT

If you buy a shiny new grill for your big day, make sure you take it out of the box and assemble it the day before; some of them take a lot of head-scratching and fiddling. In fact, you might want to take it for a test drive the weekend before your big bash, to make sure everything is in working order. Don't forget to stock up on the correct kind of charcoal or gas so you're not caught short.

"PIMP YOUR YARD"

Make sure there is plenty of shade for your guests. Check that you have enough tables, chairs, plates, cutlery, and glasses. If you are short on seats, lay out a few picnic blankets on the lawn. Burn several hours' worth of summertime music onto some CDs or create a playlist on your PC or MP3 player and rig it up to your stereo.

If you have the space, set up a few outdoor games like croquet, bocce, or badminton. If your get-together will take place in the evening, then a few details such as citronella candles will help set the mood and scare off the mosquitoes, while some rows of fairy lights will create a great atmosphere without much fuss.

THINK OF YOUR NEIGHBORS

Finally, think about the wind direction, because smoke and sound can easily travel into nearby yards and spoil your neighbors' afternoon or evening. Of course, the best way to avoid this is by inviting them to the party!

SHINE YOUR SHOES

Leather shoes need to be cleaned and polished regularly to keep them looking great and to help them last longer. If you, like us, have given your valet the year off, here are some tips from the professionals:

REMOVE DUST AND DIRT

Bang the soles of the shoes together to remove any caked-on mud, then use a damp cloth to wipe away the rest of the dust and dirt, which can easily become embedded in the leather during polishing, leaving you with an unsightly, bumpy surface.

POLISHING 101

Make sure that the polish is fresh and moist; if it's dry and cracked buy a new tin. This goes without saying, but we'll say it anyway: don't use black polish on a brown shoe, or vice versa. The polish should match the color of the shoe. Be careful not to get polish on the inside of the shoe.

APPLYING THE POLISH First, remove the laces so you can polish the tongue. Apply a small amount of polish to a small area of the shoe with a soft, lint-free cloth and work it into the leather using circular movements, pushing hard, until the surface looks cloudy. Use an old toothbrush to get into the nooks and crannies. Don't slather on too much polish; apply it in thin layers, buffing each one to a shine before applying the next.

BUFF TO A SHINE After you've covered all of the leather bits with polish, allow the shoes to dry for at least fifteen minutes to allow the nourishing oils to soak into the leather. Brush with a natural-bristle shoe-shine brush, then buff with a clean and dry soft cloth until the leather shines.

PROTECT YOUR LEATHER
To help retain their shape, use a shoe-tree insert when storing leather shoes. Treat shoes with a waterproofing spray and leather conditioner every couple of months.

> "When you have worn out your shoes, the strength of the shoe leather has passed into the fiber of your body. I measure your health by the number of shoes and hats and clothes you have worn out."
>
> —*Ralph Waldo Emerson, essayist, poet, and transcendentalist*
>
> "Make your feet your friend."
>
> —*J.M. Barrie, novelist and dramatist*

WISE MEN SAY

PLANT A TREE

There's a lot more to planting a tree than digging a hole, plopping in a sapling, and shoveling earth around the roots. It's important to consider the planting location, the time of year, the soil conditions, the size and purpose of the tree, and the care the tree will need to ensure its long-term survival.

LOCATION

Choose your site carefully. Consider the landscape: is your tree appropriate for its surroundings? Work out the maximum height and spread of the tree over its lifespan, considering the proximity of buildings and other structures. Find out how deep and wide its roots will spread so you can avoid damaging foundations or subterranean pipes and cables. Watch out for overhead phone and electrical wires, and make sure the tree won't obscure street lighting, roads, or sidewalks as it grows. If the branches of your tree grow into a neighbor's garden, he has the right to lop them off and throw them onto your side for disposal.

Ensure that as your tree grows it won't disrupt nearby habitats (such as shading them out or extracting moisture and shrinking the soil). Is the site likely to be developed in the future? Check that the soil quality (e.g., acidity/alkalinity) is suitable for the type of tree you'd like to plant.

OTHER CONSIDERATIONS:

➡ Does the tree produce poisonous fruit?

➡ Will it require ongoing maintenance, and if so who will provide it?

➡ If the land belongs to someone else, do you have his or her permission to plant on it?

➡ Does your city or county require a permit to plant a tree?

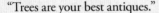

"Of all the wonders of nature, a tree in summer is perhaps the most remarkable—with the possible exception of a moose singing 'Embraceable You' in spats."

—Woody Allen, actor, comedian, playwright, and Academy Award-winning director

"Trees are your best antiques."

—Alexander Smith, essayist and poet

WISE MEN SAY

CHOICE OF SPECIES

Choose a tree that can be allowed to grow to maturity without the need for constant pruning, as this will expose it to disease. Try to copy nature, when possible, and plant a native tree or a type that is already thriving nearby.

TREE SIZE

The smaller a tree is when it is planted, the easier it will become established, because its root system will be well developed relative to its size. An older tree will take longer to settle into its new location. Choose a specimen with leading shoots, side branches, roots, and bark intact.

WHEN TO PLANT

Plant fully hardy trees any time from October to March but avoid times of severe frost. Plant half-hardy species during the spring, and palm trees during the summer. Plant hardy deciduous trees before the winter, and evergreens early or late in the season.

GET PLANTING

- Dig a hole three times the diameter of the tree's root-ball or container and deep enough that the surface of the soil around the root-ball is level with the surrounding soil.

- Before planting, give the root-ball a good soaking. If the roots are tightly compressed, tease them out using your fingers or a blunt instrument, being careful not to tear them.

- Place the root-ball in the hole and backfill around it with soil (handle larger trees by the root-ball, never the trunk). Gently shake the tree up and down to ensure good root contact with the soil, then compress gently using your hands. Tread in well around the bottom of the trunk with the sole of your foot; be careful not to overly compact heavy soil, however. Water the tree immediately, and enjoy!

IMPROVE YOUR SPELLING

Just because your computer has a spell-checker doesn't mean you should neglect your spelling. Poor spelling creates a bad impression; it's the first thing that a reader of your writing will notice and the last thing they will forget. Good spelling is no indicator of intelligence, but poor spelling sure makes you look stupid. Here are ten ways to improve:

1. The classic way to learn how to spell words correctly is to "LSCWC": look, say, cover, write, and check. This method is very effective because it engages your senses on several levels: sight, hearing, and touch, as well as reinforcing memory through repetition. The more associations you are able to make around something you wish to remember, the more neural connections you create, which is another reason this multisensory approach is so effective.

2. Read more. Everyone has particular interests. If you're not interested in reading, try reading about your interests. When you come across words that you have trouble spelling, write them down and use the LSCWC method on them later. The more you read, the better your spelling will become.

3. Keep a list of words that always cause you trouble. When you hear or read a word and are unsure of its precise meaning(s), write it down and look it up in a dictionary. Knowing a word's precise meaning(s) not only improves your chances of spelling it correctly but also sharpens your vocabulary and prevents you from using language sloppily.

4. When you are writing, always have a dictionary handy, and if you are in any doubt about the spelling, look up the word. With certain words you may even find that you are spelling them correctly, but any uncertainty will undermine your confidence and distract you from the business of writing.

5. Set aside at least an hour a week to play a spelling game such as Hangman or Scrabble. Over a year you will rack up fifty-two hours of free spelling lessons, without even realizing it!

6. Teach yourself two new words every day, one in the morning and the other before you go to bed. Over a year you will increase your vocabulary by 730 words.

7. Know your homonyms. These are words that share the same spelling or pronunciation but have different meanings, such as there/their, its/it's, too/to. Learn the rules that govern each word's use and memorize them once and for all, rather than muddling on and guessing for the rest of your life. Many grammar and spelling rules are easy; you just need to learn them properly.

8. Break words down into their syllables (the individual sounds that make up a word), and deal with them a bit at a time.

9. After you have finished a piece of writing, read it through twice to check for spelling mistakes.

10. A love of language goes hand-in-hand with a love of learning. Open yourself up to new learning experiences and don't be afraid to take on new challenges.

"Nothing you can't spell will ever work."

> —*Will Rogers, actor, humorist, and vaudevillian*

"They spell it 'Vinci' and pronounce it 'Vinchy'; foreigners always spell better than they pronounce."

> —*Mark Twain, author and satirist*

WISE MEN SAY

OPEN A STUCK JAR LID

At the top of your repertoire of manly skills should be the removal of a stubborn jar lid. Brute strength and a good grip will usually solve the problem, but here are five solutions that rely more on brains than brawn:

1. Use a triangular-tipped bottle opener to break the vacuum seal. If you won't need to reseal the jar, then simply make a hole in the top of the lid. If you want to keep the lid intact, place the triangular tip underneath the lid and lever it away from the jar until it pops.

2. Get a better grip: make sure your hands and the lid are dry, then spray some hairspray onto your hand to help it grip the lid better. Alternatively, place a small rubber mat in your palm, then twist the lid (look in the garage—there's a rubber mat on that turntable that no one uses anymore). If you don't have a rubber mat, slip on a rubber glove, or even wrap a few thick rubber bands around the lid; anything to give you better grip.

3. Tap the side of the lid with the blunt side of a knife. Sometimes this dents the metal enough to break the vacuum seal.

4. Turn the jar upside-down and give it a few firm slaps with the heel of your hand (as you would with a ketchup bottle). This loosens or breaks the seal, making the jar easier to open.

5. If the lid is made of metal, run it under hot water for a while. The lid will expand more than the glass, allowing you to unscrew it with ease. Don't use boiling water, as this could make the glass explode in your hand.

BONUS CONTAINER-OPENING TIP!

If you want to avoid being sprayed by fizz when you open a can of soda, tap the top of the can a few times with a metal spoon. This will dislodge any air bubbles that have formed there, reducing the chances of a soda explosion.

"For mad scientists who keep brains in jars, here's a tip: why not add a slice of lemon to each jar, for freshness?"

—*Jack Handey, humorist and television producer*

WISE MEN SAY

IMPRESS YOUR BOSS

I n business as in life, the best way to get is to give. If you want to get
a raise, a better job, and more responsibility and the rewards that
go with it, then you've got to be prepared to help those above and
below you. Here are ten ideas to help you impress your boss:

1. First, you've really got to believe deep down that making your boss
   look good will reflect well on you. If you are cynical and always
   assume that you are being taken for granted or exploited, then you
   are less likely to do your best to impress. If you really are being
   taken for a ride, why didn't you quit six months ago? If you're being
   treated like a doormat you've got only yourself to blame—who else
   is going to change your life but you?

2. Get over the idea that doing a good job that reflects well on your
   boss is sucking up.

3. Be cheerful, positive, and enthusiastic about whatever your boss
   asks you to do. Take pride in delivering to your boss a prestige
   service; just don't try to make anyone else look bad in the process,
   because you'll impress as much by being a team player as you would
   as a big hitter.

4. Do what you say you are going to do. Don't create expectations that
   you can't meet. Hit your deadlines and deliver what your boss ex-

pects, more if possible. This means that you have to be well prepared and have information at your fingertips, so that you can brief your boss at a moment's notice. In order to do that you have to anticipate what your boss is going to need. If you know there's an important meeting or presentation coming up, start doing the groundwork in advance on stuff that you know is a safe bet in terms of what your boss will be asking for. Your boss will be really impressed when you are able to give him what he wants on the spot because you already did it: "I already did that, because I figured you would need it."

5. Never bad-mouth your boss, even in front of people whom you think you can trust. Not only does word get around, this negativity will affect your morale and actually makes it harder for you to come up with the goods. Instead, take every opportunity to drum up your boss's good points in front of your colleagues.

6. Allow your boss to take the credit for some of your work. Give away some goodwill, and it will come back to you in spades. Don't try to grab the spotlight; a good boss will recognize your achievements without your having to jump up and down about them, and she will respect you more for your quiet professionalism.

7. Be your company's biggest fan. The higher up the hierarchy you get in a company, the more company loyalty and promotion will be expected of you, so why not get in some practice now. If you always have the company's best interests foremost in your mind, you already have the mindset of those above you. Your bosses are where they are today because they already knew this, and have been championing the company for years.

"Nothing is as embarrassing as watching your boss do something you assured him couldn't be done."

—*Earl Wilson, professional baseball player*

"The question 'Who ought to be boss?' is like asking 'Who ought to be the tenor in the quartet?' Obviously, the man who can sing tenor."

—*Henry Ford, founder of the Ford Motor Company*

WISE MEN SAY

8. Don't ask questions you can answer yourself. Your boss is too busy to spoon-feed you, so show some initiative, be resourceful, and figure stuff out for yourself sometimes. Similarly, don't approach your boss for every solution; instead, spend some time thinking about the problem and offer some solutions of your own.

9. Your boss will appreciate constructive feedback from you; if he has done something well, offering a positive response such as "I appreciated the way that you backed me up on that issue" demonstrates and reinforces how you would like to be treated.

10. If you make a mistake, don't apologize or make excuses; take responsibility for your mistakes and show that you can learn from them to do a better job next time.

TRAVEL LIGHT

Overpacking is one of the biggest mistakes a traveler can make. As a general rule, the lighter your load, the more enjoyable your journey will be. You should take half as many clothes and twice as much money.

FIVE REASONS TO PACK LIGHT

1. You won't have to worry about the airline losing your luggage.

2. If you're flying you can keep your hand luggage with you and check in later, and you won't have to wait around after the flight to collect your checked bags, because you won't have any.

3. You won't have to pay other people (like hotel porters) to carry your stuff.

4. You will be more mobile; if you need to run to make a connection you won't be slowed down by your baggage. In some airports, especially when flying on budget airlines, it can take more than thirty minutes just to walk from the check-in desk to the boarding gate.

5. You can sell your seat by volunteering to be "bumped" to the next flight, or you can become an air courier, traveling for 20 percent off regular fares in return for carrying an additional item.

"He who would travel happily must travel light."

—Antoine de Saint-Exupéry, author and aviator

"Most of my treasured memories of travel are recollections of sitting."

—Robert Thomas Allen, illustrator and portraitist

"Let your memory be your travel bag."

—Alexander Solzhenitsyn, dramatist, historian, and Noble Prize-winning novelist

WISE MEN SAY

WHAT TO TAKE—AND WHAT TO LEAVE AT HOME

- ◆ If you think, "I may need this," you probably won't; if it's more like, "I can't survive without this," you better pack it.

- ◆ Bring a small container of laundry soap for washing clothes by hand, which will greatly decrease the amount of clothes you'll need to pack. Choose fabrics that will dry quickly (i.e., overnight).

- ◆ Your mom was right! Rather than packing heavy, bulky clothes for cold climates, keep warm by layering. A pair of thermal long johns plus a pair of jeans is lighter than a heavy coat.

- If you will be traveling for a long time, pack some older clothes that you won't mind throwing away during your trip. This will lighten your load—or at least allow room for souvenirs.

- Choose your socks and underwear carefully. They need to last because they can be among the most difficult items to replace in certain parts of the world. Cotton socks are a bad choice because they absorb moisture, rather than wicking moisture away from the skin. Synthetic fibers will keep your feet comfortable and dry. Wool blends are okay, but they don't wear well. Avoid synthetic underwear, however, which doesn't breathe.

- Never pack new shoes that you haven't worn. Take only shoes that you have already "broken in."

- If you're going somewhere sunny, pack a light, soft, floppy sun hat that protects the back of your neck. If the climate is cold, take a knit cap.

- A few items you shouldn't leave behind: an alarm clock, a compact flashlight, an inflatable travel pillow, a sewing kit, insect repellent, sunscreen, and copies of important documents.

PLAY POKER LIKE A PRO

We're assuming you know how to play poker. If not, that's great; it means you don't have any bad habits to unlearn, so go away and learn the rules, then come back and read these nine pro poker tips.

Before we begin, here are the odds that you're playing against: there are 2,598,960 possible poker hands in a 52-card deck.

Rank of hands	Number of possible ways hand can be made	Chance of being dealt in original 5 Cards
Royal flush	4	1 in 649,740.00
Straight flush	36	1 in 72,193.33
Four of a kind	624	1 in 4,165.00
Full house	3,744	1 in 694.16
Flush	5,108	1 in 508.80
Straight	10,200	1 in 254.80
Three of a kind	54,912	1 in 47.32
Two pairs	123,552	1 in 21.03
One pair	1,098,240	1 in 2.36
No-pair hand	1,302,540	1 in 1.99

1. In poker, as in many other forms of combat and competition, it is always preferable to take a defensive position and let your opponent try to beat you, rather than trying to beat them. Then you can turn their energy and momentum against them.

2. Don't enter a game unless you have a bankroll that is at least fifty times the table limit. If your bankroll is growing, exercise self-control and don't blow it by getting greedy and playing too high too fast. If the table limit suits your bankroll, and you are making money slowly, that doesn't mean you will make money any faster by switching to a game with a higher limit, which could mean you will lose faster.

"The commonest mistake in history is underestimating your opponent; it happens at the poker table all the time."

—*David M. Shoup, general and former commandant, U.S. Marine Corps*

"Whether he likes it or not, a man's character is stripped at the poker table; if the other players read him better than he does, he has only himself to blame. Unless he is both able and prepared to see himself as others do, flaws and all, he will be a loser in cards, as in life."

—*Anthony Holden, journalist, broadcaster, and biographer*

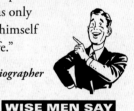

WISE MEN SAY

3. Mediocre players play inside their comfort zone, which means they usually fall into particular patterns of behavior. If you can recognize these patterns, you can exploit them.

4. Figure out your opponents' "tells": the unconscious signs they make when they're anxious or lying (remember *Casino Royale*?). Get a friend to figure out some of yours, so that you can double-bluff by faking tells. But remember, disguising or faking your feelings badly is worse than showing them.

5. Pick your battles: play for the long haul, rather than making a fast buck. Don't try to win every hand. It is better to win six small pots than one big one.

6. Try to play with worse players than you. When gambling is involved, why reduce your chances of winning by playing out of your depth?

7. In general, if you've got a poor hand, fold quickly; if you've got a good hand, make other players cough up some big bucks to see your cards.

8. The odds of improving your hand on the draw are about 50/50.

9. Make sure the reward is worth the risk. If you have a 1 in 13 chance of making an inside straight, don't get hung up on making the straight if the rewards do not outweigh the risks.

ADVANCED DRIVING SKILLS

One of the most effective ways to become a better driver is to brush up on your regular driving skills first by, for example, checking your mirrors before every maneuver and observing the correct stopping distance and speed limits, etc. That done, here are some more advanced driving tips:

REDUCE YOUR BLIND SPOT

Sometimes advanced driving involves setting up the car correctly. Most people position their side mirrors so that they can see the road behind them from a normal sitting position. Any driver knows that there is a blind spot between the rear-view mirror and the side mirror, which is why it's safest to glance over your shoulder before you change lanes. You can reduce the blind spot, however, by setting up your side mirrors differently: sit in the driver's seat and lean up against the door; place your head against the window and move the mirror until you can see along the side of the vehicle. Then sit in the passenger's seat and do the same with its side mirror. Now you will find that when a car disappears from your rear-view mirror it will appear almost immediately in your side mirror.

BENDS

When driving along an unfamiliar, winding road, gauge the sharpness of the bends by looking at trees, hedges, streetlights, and buildings along the side of the road. Increase your view of the bend by positioning the car to the left on a right-hand turn, and vice versa on a left-hand turn.

SPEED

Use "limit point analysis" to assess your speed. If the farthest point you can see ahead of you appears to be getting farther away, your speed is probably okay. If the point is getting closer, however, slow down until it stays the same and then starts appearing farther away.

"Your grandchildren will likely find it incredible—or even sinful—that you burned up a gallon of gasoline to fetch a pack of cigarettes!"

—Paul B. MacCready Jr., PhD, aeronautical engineer and inventor

"When buying a used car, punch the buttons on the radio. If all the stations are rock and roll, there's a good chance the transmission is shot."

—Larry Lujack, disc jockey

"The one thing that unites all human beings, regardless of age, gender, religion, economic status, or ethnic background, is that, deep down inside, we ALL believe that we are above-average drivers."

—Dave Barry, author and Pulitzer Prize-winning humorist

WISE MEN SAY

ANTILOCK BRAKES

If you have antilock brakes, you don't need to pump them during an emergency stop. Simply jam your foot down hard on the brake and leave it there. You will feel a grinding sensation through the brake pedal; this is the antilock brake system rapidly switching your brakes on and off to prevent the car from skidding.

DRIVING ON ICE

When the road is icy, drive in a high gear and use the engine to slow the vehicle down, rather than the brakes. This reduces the possibility of a skid.

FUEL EFFICIENCY

Advanced driving and fuel efficiency go hand-in-hand. Have you ever been stuck traveling between 30 and 60 miles per hour amid traffic that forces you to brake and accelerate repeatedly? This uses a lot of gas. But you can decrease your fuel consumption and reduce your brake wear by trying to maintain a constant speed and anticipating when you will need to slow down, so that you can ease off the accelerator instead of using the brake.

BRAIN FOOD

A man dressed all in black is walking down the road. He is wearing a black coat, black shoes, a black shirt, a black scarf, black pants, and a black ski mask covers his face. He is carrying a flashlight, but the batteries are dead. A black car comes around the corner at high speed, with its lights turned off, but the driver manages to brake in time. How did the driver see the man?

Solution: It was daytime.

THE BIGGER PICTURE

Many drivers fail to look far enough ahead, and instead zone out on a spot about twenty-five yards away. Keep your eyes moving so that you can take in the bigger picture. Always assume that everyone else is incompetent; that way your brain will always be alert and anticipating a variety of possible hazards ahead. For example, every time you pass someone on a freeway, assume that they haven't seen you and that at any moment they could pull out in front of you again without signaling.

GET SERVED IN A CROWDED BAR

Becoming impatient, shouting "What do you need to do to get served in this joint?" or flirting are three of the best ways to get labeled a jerk by a bartender, and will only increase the length of time you have to wait before slaking your thirst. If you want to get your drinks faster than the average barfly, next time you belly-up try some of these tricks:

- Tip the first time, the second time, and every other time after that! If there's one thing that features big on a bar person's radar, it's a guy who gave a fat, juicy tip the last time around.

- Be pleasant; staying calm and smiling amiably increases your chances of getting served quickly. No one wants to serve a grouch. Don't whistle or wave cash in the air. Would you do your job any faster with some idiot thrusting his wad in your face?

- Women usually get served quicker at bars by male bartenders than guys do, and even when the bar staff are female there is a marginal difference. Short of having a gender reassignment, there's not much you can do about this. As a guy, however, you can position yourself next to a woman and, while she is getting served, catch the eye of the bar person and smile and nod while pointing at the woman he or she is serving. This is a polite way of saying, "Serve me next?" Avoid the barman stud-muffin who wants to serve only attractive females, however, because he's not the slightest bit interested in serving you.

- Stand next to or across from the cash register. Bar staff always have to return to it at the end of most rounds.

- Lean forward over the bar at no more than a 30-degree angle—any more and you'll look pushy; any less and you'll look content to wait it out for a while. Bar staff want to keep their clients happy, so if someone looks too content, they'll serve someone who wants it more.

- Tall people get served more quickly than short people do. Stand on tiptoe, if necessary, and try to make your head stand out above the thirsty masses.

- Avoid the dead areas at the end of a long bar, where the crowd is thinnest. You may be attracted by the empty space, but it's empty for a reason: no one will take any notice of you over there.

- Have your money ready and know what you want to order. In a busy bar there's nothing more irritating than a ditherer who takes ages to count out his change.

- Order several drinks at a time; believe it or not, bartenders are quite capable of remembering a long list of drinks—it's what they do every day. They won't thank you for requiring them to make several return trips as you rattle out your order one agonizing drink after another.

- Become a regular; the more hours you put in on the drinking side of the bar, the more easily you will get recognized by the bar staff. But don't assume you're a regular until you know the bar staff by name, and they know yours.

"The problem with the world is that everyone is a few drinks behind."

—Humphrey Bogart, Academy Award-winning actor

"I envy people who drink. At least they have something to blame everything on."

—Oscar Levant, actor, author, comedian, and composer

WISE MEN SAY

GET THE BEST TABLE IN A RESTAURANT

Apart from being rich and famous, there's no big secret to getting excellent service at a swanky restaurant, and that includes bagging the best table. It all comes down to planning ahead, while treating yourself and others with courtesy and respect.

- Plan well ahead and reserve a table as early as possible. Some of the coolest restaurants have a waiting list stretching into several months, so if you can book a few months in advance, you've won half the battle. Comment on how good the food was on your last visit. (If you haven't been there before, make something up!) You'll come across as polite and complimentary, rather than sounding like a newbie.

- Don't ask straight out for the best table in the house; it makes you sound arrogant, and you aren't giving them a good reason to give it to you. If you're celebrating a special occasion, mention it to the maître d' when you make your reservation and explain how you really want the

evening to go perfectly. This establishes that you have an expectation of special service, without spelling it out in a crude and bullying way. Nevertheless, you've demonstrated that you take your requirements seriously. Ask his advice about the best tables. This places him in the role of expert adviser; he will be more inclined to assist you because you have raised his status.

- Phone the restaurant immediately if the size of your party changes.

- Confirm the reservation before you arrive. The last thing you want is to be waiting in the loser line with guests you want to impress.

- Be well groomed: dress to kill to demonstrate that you respect yourself and have some class. How can you expect to be held in high esteem if you look like you belong in a fast-food joint? If in doubt, overdress.

- Turn up on time and introduce yourself to the maître d'. Explain who you are and remind him of the conversation you had about your special occasion. At the end of the evening, thank him again and send your compliments to the chef. Needless to say, tip generously and next time you will receive even better service.

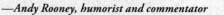

"I went to a restaurant that serves 'breakfast at any time.' So I ordered French toast during the Renaissance."

—Steven Wright, stand-up comedian, actor, and author

"Never trust the food in a restaurant on top of the tallest building in town that spends a lot of time folding napkins."

—Andy Rooney, humorist and commentator

WISE MEN SAY

HIT A GOLF BALL

What can be so hard about hitting a stationary ball? In most other sports the ball is moving, and you're probably running at the same time. So why so many air shots, hooks, slices, and other disasters? In golf, more than in just about any other sport, you've got to be thinking the right thoughts to hit a good shot. For instance, common sense would suggest that, if you want to hit a ball into the air, you would need to hit it up. In fact, in golf you have to think of hitting down; better still, think of swinging the club smoothly and letting the ball get in the way. Eventually, the swing will be so fixed in your muscle memory that you won't have to think at all.

THE GRIP

❖ Close the fingers of your left hand around the grip, with your thumb on top and pointing down the shaft. Place the crease of your right hand over your left hand so that your left thumb fits into the crease, while the index finger and thumb of your right hand are holding the grip. Hold the club lightly with both hands. (Reverse these directions if you're left-handed.)

THE DRIVE

- Stand facing the ball with your left shoulder (right if you are left-handed) pointing in the direction you want the ball to travel. Your feet should be shoulder width apart, your knees slightly bent (not locked). Your hands should be slightly ahead of the ball.

- Your main focus should be on the target. Yes, you need to look at the ball as you make the shot, but don't think about the clubface hitting the ball. Don't rush your swing, because you'll sacrifice balance for speed and end up with a poor shot.

- At the start of the backswing your weight should be evenly distributed between the heels and balls of both feet; at the end of the backswing most of your weight should be on your right foot; at impact about 75 percent should be on your left foot, and about 90 percent by the end of the follow-through.

"I'm about five inches from being an outstanding golfer. That's the distance my left ear is from my right."

—*Ben Crenshaw, professional golfer*

"Golf combines two favorite American pastimes: taking long walks and hitting things with a stick."

—*P.J. O'Rourke, journalist, satirist, and author*

WISE MEN SAY

- Keep your right hand straight for as long as possible without cocking your wrist. Your left arm provides the power, while control comes through your right arm. Keep your left arm straight during the swing. Thinking about throwing an underhand ball will give you an idea of the action involved in driving a golf ball. Where does your head and body end up after you throw a ball? Facing the target. It's the same with the golf swing.

THE PUTT

- Stand facing the ball with your weight evenly balanced, and putt with your head as far behind the ball as comfortably possible.

- Make several practice strokes while standing next to the ball.

- When you putt, keep the face of the putter square with the target line at all times.

- Don't ram the ball into the hole; think instead of trying to get the ball as close to the hole as possible, and concentrate on the line and speed of the ball.

- Think of the putter acting as a pendulum hanging within a triangle formed by your arms and shoulders. When you putt, keep your head down while looking at the ball, rather than looking up to see where it's going.

TOBACCO

QUIT SMOKING

Quitting smoking can be one of the hardest things you'll ever have to do in your life. There are lot of ways to make it easier, however, and it begins with knowing what smoking does to your body, making proper preparations before quitting, and being able to recognize the symptoms of withdrawal.

WHAT ARE THE EFFECTS OF SMOKING?

The immediate effects are an increase in blood pressure and heart rate; the blood flow to your extremities is decreased. Your brain and nervous system will be briefly stimulated but then depressed. Your appetite is depressed, along with your sense of taste and smell.

The long-term effects include shortness of breath; persistent cough; reduced fitness; stained fingers and teeth; depressed immune system; decreased fertility; prematurely aged skin; lung infections such as pneumonia and bronchitis; emphysema; heart attack and coronary disease; cancers of the lung, throat, mouth, bladder, kidney, and pancreas; stomach ulcers; and death.

READY TO QUIT YET?

Preparation is the key to quitting. Draw a line down the middle of a large piece of paper. On the left-hand side list all of the reasons for smoking; on the right-hand side list all of the reasons for and benefits of quitting.

Throw or give away all of your cigarettes, lighters, pipes, cigars, and other smoking paraphernalia such as rolling machines. Tell everyone who will listen that you are quitting. The more people you tell, the harder it will be to let yourself down.

RECOGNIZE THE SYMPTOMS OF WITHDRAWAL

Nicotine is a powerful drug, and kicking the habit will result in some unpleasant withdrawal symptoms. Recognizing those symptoms goes a long way toward overcoming them without relapsing.

ANXIETY, ANGER, IRRITABILITY, RESTLESSNESS, REDUCED ENERGY

Nicotine hijacks various hormone systems within your body, including that of adrenaline and insulin, as well as feel-good chemicals such as dopamine, serotonin, and noradrenaline. Your body will need time to readjust itself to the processes it used to control these chemicals before you became a smoker.

Nicotine triggers the release of stored fat into the bloodstream, which is why smoking a cigarette can give you an instant sugar rush (and also why it clogs your arteries). Without this prop, you'll need to maintain healthy blood-sugar levels by eating regular meals, reducing your caffeine intake, and drinking lots of water to flush out the toxins.

TIME DRAGS WHEN YOU CAN'T TAKE A DRAG A recent study has shown that time-perception distortion is a common recovery symptom while quitting smoking. Cravings last for only about three minutes at a time, even though they can feel like they last an eternity. Check your watch at the beginning of a craving episode to give yourself a realistic perception of time, otherwise you will feel like you're dealing with the anxiety of craving continually.

POOR CONCENTRATION This symptom is reported by about two-thirds of quitters and is associated with low blood sugar, as your body gets used to regulating your blood-sugar level without the aid of nicotine.

CAN'T STOP EATING Many smokers report an increased appetite and weight gain. Nicotine suppressed your appetite by delivering stored fat and sugar into your bloodstream whenever you wanted it; the increased hunger during recovery is most likely caused by your erratic eating habits, which didn't bother you when you were smoking. Now that you no longer have the quick-fix sugar rush that nicotine provided, it is essential that you eat regular, healthy meals.

CAN'T SLEEP Your body is re-establishing "normal" sleeping patterns, as well as returning to your true level of need. You may even require less sleep than you did previously. Also, remember that caffeine is metabolized twice as fast by non-smokers, so if you are still drinking lots of coffee, it's the equivalent of doubling your caffeine intake—no wonder you can't sleep.

CHEST TIGHTNESS, SORE THROAT, AND COUGHING Your lungs are ridding themselves of years of tar buildup, and the little bronchial hairs are growing back and becoming sensitive again. Your throat is healing. Drinking water will help ease this cleansing process.

HEADACHES Your blood-oxygen and sugar levels are changing, and you are experiencing the stress of quitting, plus your caffeine level may need reducing.

RECOGNIZE YOUR TRIGGERS

Your subconscious is not very tenacious about demanding fulfillment of a craving. If you can hold out for about three minutes, your subconscious simply gives up (and tries again later). Likewise, if you avoid or resist your triggers—the places, situations, and activities—that make you want to smoke, those triggers quickly cease to be effective. After your first week on the wagon, expect your "let's celebrate" trigger to make you crave a cigarette.

THRIVING, NOT DEPRIVING

Concentrate on the positive benefits you're gaining as a result of not smoking, rather than dwelling on feelings of being deprived of a cigarette.

DON'T BLAME THE BUTTS

It is important not to blame the lack of cigarettes for your feelings, moods, or emotions. Your mind and body are always looking for an excuse to relapse. If you encounter a crisis, remember that having a cigarette will not help you deal with the crisis any more efficiently. It will simply add another problem (your smoking again) to your existing crisis.

MOW THE LAWN

Having a lawn that looks like a putting green is an impossible dream unless you employ a team of landscapers to mow and water daily, and make it your full-time obsession. Nevertheless, here's how to get the best perf from your turf without having to give up your day job:

- At the beginning of the mowing season, sharpen (or replace, if necessary) the blades on your lawnmower. Sharp blades give the optimum cut. Check the oil and gas levels. Rake out dead grass, aerate your lawn, and re-seed bare patches.

- Before mowing, examine the lawn and remove any large sticks or non-grass items (especially rocks, which will damage the blade).

- Grass is stimulated to grow by being cut, so if you mow it infrequently it will grow less vigorously. Regular mowing is better for the grass than letting it grow long. In the height of the growing season you should cut it twice a week, weather permitting.

- Mow the lawn only when the grass is dry, unless continual rain has prevented you from cutting it for several weeks. Wet lawn clippings create unsightly clumps and allow the spread of a disease that harms the grass. Wet clippings also tend to get stuck inside the roof of the mower and can clog up the blade, and should be scraped away when they are dry.

- Don't cut the grass too short, as short grass sends out a smaller root system that fares less well during times of drought. Remove only about a third of the height of the grass at a time. Mow very long grass in two or three stages over the course of a week, rather than trying to mow it all at once.

- Mow around the edge of the lawn first. This gives you a border in which to maneuver when you turn the mower at the end of each row. Then mow up and down the lawn to create those enviable stripes (which will look their best if your mower has a roller). Don't always cut in the same direction. Mow up and down the lawn one week, side to side the next, and diagonally from time to time.

- If the mower runs out of gas in mid-mow, wait for a few minutes for the engine to cool down before removing the gas cap. If you have an electric mower, use a circuit breaker (sling the cable over your shoulder and keep it behind you while you mow). Start at the side of the lawn nearest the power source and work your way out.

- Keep cutting the grass into the fall months, and give it one last cut after it has stopped growing, so that the grass is about an inch shorter than usual; this will help it to overwinter.

"A perfect summer day is when the sun is shining, the breeze is blowing, the birds are singing, and the lawn mower is broken."

—*James Dent, humor columnist*

"There's one good thing about snow, it makes your lawn look as nice as your neighbor's."

—*Clyde Moore, business executive*

WISE MEN SAY

PITCH A CURVEBALL

Most anyone can pitch a baseball, but getting an awesome curve is one of the hardest and most physically demanding skills in the game. Work on your regular fast pitch, as that will be your staple, but when you want to mix things up a bit, throw in a curveball every once in a while.

WHAT IS A CURVEBALL?

A curveball is a slower than average pitch with topspin; it looks as if it's heading straight for home plate, but as it gets close to the batter it moves down and to the left or right as much as sixteen inches. If it's really good it will force the batter to jump out of its way.

HOW DOES IT WORK?

The ball curves because of a phenomenon called the Magnus effect (named for German physicist Heinrich Gustav Magnus, who first described the effect in 1853). The ball creates a kind of whirlpool of rotating air around itself. As the ball travels through the air, it meets more resistance at the top of the ball than at the bottom, so that the air moves faster around the bottom of the ball than at the top, and it is this low pressure at the bottom that makes the ball fall sharply downward. It's the same principle that gives an airplane lift.

HEALTH WARNING

Most baseball coaches advise that only pitchers who have reached physical maturity should attempt to throw curveballs, as it puts a lot of strain on the shoulder, elbow, and wrist. In Little League, it's almost impossible to throw a curveball anyway, because there isn't enough distance between the pitcher and the batter.

THE CURVEBALL GRIP

Grip the ball by placing your middle finger and index finger closely together on the inside half of the seam, with your ring and pinkie fingers resting under the ball, with only the pinkie actually touching it. The side of your thumb should be on top of the seam; your thumb and middle fingers should be in contact with a seam. Don't rest the ball in your palm. Squeeze with your middle finger and thumb to maintain a firm grip on the ball, keeping the index finger relaxed.

THE PITCH

Use the same pitching action you would for an ordinary pitch but bend your wrist back on the windup. At the end of the pitch, curve your wrist down quickly and away to the side (don't "snap" or "twist" your wrist—think more in terms of pulling down a window shade or of an ax-chopping motion).

After releasing the ball, follow through with your arm by bending your wrist so that the back of your hand ends up facing the batter.

> "I was planning to be a baseball player until I ran into something called a curveball. And that set me back."
>
> —*Ben Chandler III, U.S. congressman*
>
> "The story of the curveball is the story of the game itself. Some would say of life itself."
>
> —*Martin Quigley, author of* The Crooked Pitch

WISE MEN SAY

SHOOT A FREE THROW

Being able to sink a free throw is one of those skills you pull out every now and then to amaze your friends or take home the prize at a free-throw contest. If you've got the air-ball blues, however, the eight tips below will help to ensure you'll get nothin' but net from now on.

1. Stand just behind the free-throw line, feet shoulder width apart, with one foot slightly farther forward than the other, if that feels more comfortable.

2. Your upper body should be square with the basket, and your lead foot (same side as your shooting arm) should be lined up directly with the center of the rim (look for the nail or dot at the middle of the free-throw line).

3. You have ten seconds to shoot the ball, so bounce it a couple of times or do whatever you have to do to loosen up. Once you've found a pre-throw preparation that works for you, use it every time, otherwise you will never achieve consistency.

4. If you shoot with your right hand, support the weight of the ball and hold it steady with the fingertips of your left hand. Place the middle three fingers of your shooting hand around the ball. Hold the ball in your fingers, not your palms.

5. Keeping your shooting arm straight, cock your wrist back and line up the ball to aim just above the rim. Bring the elbow of your shooting arm beneath the ball, and lift the ball to a comfortable shoulder height.

6. Keep your eye on the target throughout the shot.

7. Bend your knees and make the shot by straightening them again to propel your body upward. This provides most of the thrust for the shot, not your shooting arm, although your arm certainly produces some of the thrust. Just before the top of the "jump," release the ball with your fingertips and snap your wrist forward to produce some backspin on the ball.

8. Continue to follow through with your shooting hand, as if you were reaching into the rim. At the end of the shot you should be standing on your toes.

Once you have perfected the technique, the rest of the battle is a mental one. Clear your mind before each free throw and concentrate only on the ball going through the hoop. Then keep practicing until you become a free-throwing machine!

"I look at the NBA as a football game without the helmet."

—*Tom Tolbert, professional basketball player and commentator*

"The only difference between a good shot and a bad shot is if it goes in or not."

—*Charles Barkley, professional basketball player and MVP*

WISE MEN SAY

ORDER AND EAT SUSHI

If you don't like sushi, chances are you haven't eaten at a good enough sushi bar yet. So digest these pointers, then give it another try! Eating at a sushi bar isn't cheap, but price is not necessarily an indicator of quality; above all look for a place that is full of Japanese people.

Probably the most important factor you should consider when eating sushi is the considerable amount of skill and time that goes into the preparation of these exquisite bundles of flavor. Eat sushi at the bar (the only place to get the full sushi experience). Eat slowly, and take time to savor its subtle interplay of textures and flavors. For the uninitiated, the tips below will take the mystery out of ordering and enjoying sushi.

CHEF KNOWS BEST

Ask the sushi chef to recommend his choice of fish (he should offer you the freshest). Order one kind of sushi at a time (two or three only if the bar is really busy). Sushi comes in pairs, so every time you order one thing you will receive two anyway!

Before you eat, the server will bring you a hot towel called an oshibori. Use it to wipe your hands before you touch any food.

CHOPSTICK ETIQUETTE

Wooden chopsticks will be joined together; snap them apart, and rub cheap chopsticks together to remove any splinters (but don't rub good quality chopsticks together, as this is insulting).

When you are not eating, place the chopsticks in front of you and parallel to the edge of the sushi bar. Don't place them directly on the bar; rest the ends on the small ceramic block (called the hashi oki).

Don't stick or dip chopsticks vertically into any food, especially rice. Hold your chopsticks at an angle. When helping yourself from a communal plate, use the reverse, fatter ends of the chopsticks (the other ends have been in your mouth). Don't pass food with your chopsticks or use them to feed someone else. Put the entire contents of one chopstick-full into your mouth (don't bite off a piece and then return the rest to your plate).

GARI AND WASABI

Every sushi order comes with a serving of pickled ginger (gari) and a small mound of wasabi (hot, green horseradish). Use the ginger as a palette cleanser between sushi dishes. Mix the wasabi with soy sauce to your taste.

The soy is supposed to flavor the fish, not the rice, so avoid dipping the rice into the soy, as it will affect the delicate aroma and flavor and make the rice soggy. Also, don't dip anything that already has a sauce into the soy.

Leaving food is considered rude, especially rice. Never leave rice. Soup is drunk straight from the bowl, and it's acceptable to slurp.

TIPPING

At the end of your meal, give the bulk of your tip to the sushi chef and the rest to the servers.

FIVE WARNING SIGNS THAT YOU SHOULD TRY A BETTER SUSHI BAR

1. The fish is not on display.

2. The food looks dry.

3. You're not able to order only one or two dishes at a time, and have to place a multiple order all in one shot, or are encouraged to pay a fixed price for all you can eat.

4. The sushi rice is bland, and the majority of the ingredients are cooked (rather than raw).

5. The menu is written only in English (a sign that Japanese people don't eat there).

BIG-PAY
POSITIONS

KEEP OUT

College
Men Only

TWELVE INTERVIEW TIPS

Knowing how to conduct yourself in an interview is crucial for your career prospects and your subsequent standard of living. Do you know the twelve steps to interview success?

1. Do your research: discover everything you can about the company, and make sure the information is up to date. Check out the company literature and its website. If you know someone who works there, pick their brains about the direction in which the company wants to move, the company ethos, its areas of strength and weakness, etc. Find out what you can about the interviewers. If you don't know anything about the company, how can the interviewer believe that you want to work there or that you could be an asset to the company? Continue to gather information during the interview.

2. Anticipate the questions you will be asked in the interview and practice your responses. Don't just think you can wing it and impress them with your spontaneity. Interviewers want to employ people who take the trouble to prepare, rather than lazy guys who try to get away with the absolute minimum. Prepare to answer open-ended questions such as "Tell me a little about yourself," as these are the hardest to answer off the cuff.

3. Be on time: plan to arrive at least half an hour before the interview. Have a cup of coffee across the street to gather your thoughts.

4. Don't talk too much. Many a candidate has talked their way out of a job by giving away too much information. It is important to listen to the question, then keep your answer brief and to the point—two to three minutes maximum. You should speak for about one-third of the interview and certainly no more than half.

> "When you go in for a job interview, I think a good thing to ask is if they ever press charges."
>
> *—Jack Handey, humorist and television producer*

> "Never wear a backward baseball cap to an interview unless applying for the job of umpire."
>
> *—Dan Zevin, humorist and author*

WISE MEN SAY

5. Be enthusiastic and positive. Even if you hate your existing job, don't make negative comments about it. Instead, try to find the positives and the challenges it has offered you.

6. Make regular eye contact. If you are the kind of person who thinks by allowing their eyes to scan a room or fix upward, you'll need to consciously work on looking at other people in the eye while you are talking to them.

7. Focus on results rather than qualities. You may have a list of great qualities, but they count for nothing if you are unable to demonstrate how you have achieved positive results in the past.

8. Treat the interview as an opportunity to see whether you want the job. This will encourage you to ask intelligent and incisive questions, and will make you feel less like you are begging for a job. Think in terms of testing a mutual compatibility, rather than going all-out to impress.

9. The first rule of sales is to find out what the "customer" wants. It's the same with an interview; you are selling yourself, so ask the interviewers what they are looking for: "What are you most hoping to find in the person you hire?" or "What would be my top priorities on the job?" are great questions.

10. If you lack a particular skill, emphasize how quickly you are prepared to learn; give an example of a time when you have learned quickly on the job.

11. Don't be the first to raise the subject of money. Wait until after you have been offered the job before getting into detailed discussions about salary.

12. Be honest; there is no point in talking your way into a job that you are incapable of doing, or that you won't enjoy. The more honest you are, the greater the chance that you'll find a job that really suits your needs.

PREPARE A ROMANTIC DINNER

The best way to be romantic is to go the extra mile, make that special bit of effort that she won't expect, demonstrating to her that she deserves your singular attention to detail. Anything that shows you've taken extra care to make the evening special will score you bonus points. And if you manage to successfully pull off an entire meal without disaster, her heart will be yours.

SET THE MOOD

This is the part that requires you to turn your stinking bachelor pad into an oasis of amorousness, a palace of passion, so for heaven's sake clean up a bit. Open some windows to give the place a good airing, gather up all the dirty laundry behind the sofa and stash it somewhere out of sight, and clear away the pizza boxes and empty bottles of beer from last night's session with the guys. Buy a big bouquet of flowers and put them in a vase in a prominent place.

Half an hour before she arrives, dim the lights, put on some romantic music, and light plenty of candles. Go for tall candles over tea lights; it's more flattering to be lit from above. Avoid scented candles until after the meal, because you don't want to ruin the delicate flavors of the culinary taste sensation you are preparing in the kitchen. Once you've eaten, there's everything to be gained by lighting a vanilla, lavender, or jasmine candle to arouse the senses.

STICK TO THE TRIED AND TRUE

Don't try a new dish for the first time on your special evening. Stick to what you know, otherwise when it all goes wrong you'll be sending out for pizza again, like last night, only this time you'll be eating it on your own.

THINK AHEAD

Do as much prep as you can before you start cooking, like chopping vegetables or preparing a first course. Have all of your ingredients at hand, so you don't have to dive to the back of a kitchen cupboard at a crucial moment. When she arrives you'll need to be calm and in control, rather than flinging her coat on the sofa, thrusting a drink into her hand, and running back into the kitchen to stop the meal from burning. Stress-free cooking will ensure that you both have a relaxing and enjoyable evening.

IMPRESS WITHOUT STRESS

Instead of serving an appetizer, consider splurging on a few carefully selected cheeses and some good olives served with sliced pear and grapes and a baguette. These are foolproof, impressive, and require little preparation. Once you sit down to eat you don't want to be fussing over the cooking—you want to be able to give her your full attention. Choose a main course, such as lasagna, that can bake unattended in the oven while the two of you nibble on the cheese and olives and sip glasses of wine or an aperitif. Pair it with a tossed green salad, and you're set.

For dessert, you can keep things simple by buying something from a reliable bakery, or serve a scoop of gourmet ice cream with a few upscale packaged cookies on the side.

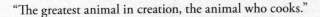

"The greatest animal in creation, the animal who cooks."

—*Douglas Jerrold, dramatist and author*

WISE MEN SAY

GET PERFECT ABS

What man doesn't want washboard abs and a lean, ripped body? Being ripped means combining good muscle mass with a percentage of total body fat between 12 and 14.5 percent, which is quite low when you consider that even some competition-ready professional bodybuilders have up to 9 percent body fat, while a "healthy" and normal range would be between 14 and 20 percent for Mr. Average (it will be higher if he is overweight).

Already we can see that getting beach-ready is no walk in the park. It takes proper nutrition and plenty of cardio and weight training. No amount of sit-ups and crunches will give you ripped abs. The only way to do it is to lose the fat. Here are the things that you must focus on:

EAT RIGHT

This is more important than any other factor; get your diet right, and the rest will fall into place. If your diet is poor, you'll lack the necessary energy and motivation to begin exercising, and you won't lose body fat.

- Keep your daily caloric intake between 2,000 and 2,500 calories (unless you are training really hard); increase your protein intake and don't eat anything after 6 p.m.

- Reduce salt, sugar, and simple carbohydrates and drink at least eight glasses of water each day.

- Don't starve yourself, or your metabolism will slow down and fat-burning will cease.

- Don't eliminate the fat; consume between 50 to 80 grams daily. Good sources of fat include fish oils, egg yolks, olive oil, flax or almond oil, and avocados. Steer clear of saturated, hydrogenated, and trans fats.

EXERCISE

If you're not following a good diet, then exercise alone will not give you the desired results. Half an hour of cardiovascular exercise every day will burn fat. The longer and more intense the cardio, the greater will be the fat loss. Work in three half-hour sessions of resistance exercise (weight training) each week.

Make your training your priority and fit in your other interests and commitments around it; that way you won't be tempted to slope off when the going gets tough—you'll simply accept it as part of your daily routine.

GET LOTS OF REST

If your body can't recover it won't benefit, so don't overdo the exercise, or you'll end up losing muscle mass rather than fat. Focus on your whole body, not just your abs. Rest each muscle group for forty-eight hours between sessions (e.g., train your legs on Monday, Wednesday, and Friday; upper body on Tuesday, Thursday, and Saturday). Rest for a minute between each set.

"Start by doing what's necessary, then what's possible, and suddenly you are doing the impossible."

—*Francis of Assisi, Roman Catholic friar and patron saint of animals*

"There is no great achievement that is not the result of patient working and waiting."

—*J.G. Holland, novelist and poet*

WISE MEN SAY

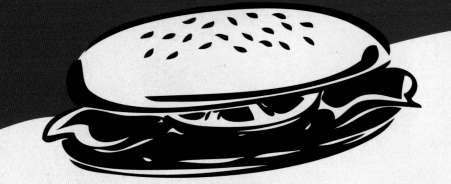

MAKE THE PERFECT BURGER

Run as far away as you can from those tasteless, artery-clogging excuses for burgers that you can buy at any fast-food joint. Don't you know that you're missing out on a whole world of fat, juicy, home-cooked burgers?

IT'S ALL IN THE PATTY

The key to the perfect burger is in the patty, which is usually made of beef. It is vital, however, that you go to a small, local butcher (if you can find one) and ask them to choose the meat they consider best for the job, then have them grind it coarsely. The butcher will know that the meat needs to be at least 7 percent fat, otherwise the cooked burger will be dry. The coarse grind helps the burger to stick together; if the mince is too fine, the burger will crumble during cooking. Mince the meat yourself only if you have a proper mincer—cutting the meat finely with a knife just won't do.

When you get home, place about a pound and a half of minced meat in a large bowl and add one large onion, finely chopped, a teaspoon of salt, half a teaspoon of pepper, two tablespoons of bottled barbecue sauce, and two cloves of garlic, finely chopped (some people like to sauté the chopped onion and garlic before adding it to the chopped beef).

Use your hands to mix the ingredients together (don't overwork the mixture), then split into six quarter-pound balls.

Flatten each quarter-pounder, then place them in the refrigerator to firm up. If you cook them immediately they are likely to fall apart, as the heat from your hands will warm the mixture to more than room temperature.

COOKING

If you are using an overhead grill or one of those clamshell grilling machines, turn to the hottest setting. You want the meat to seal quickly in order to retain the juices. Cook each burger for six minutes, flipping after three. They are ready to eat when the juices run clear and the burger feels firm.

THE BUN

You can't beat a soft, white burger bun, topped with sesame seeds, as long as it is fresh. Cut the bun in half and toast lightly. Then add the cooked burger and a whole heap of fresh fixings: finely chopped lettuce, tomato, pickles, relish, mayo, whatever.

OTHER MEATS

A burger doesn't have to be made out of beef! Why not try pork, turkey, lamb, a veggie patty, or a mixture of meat (50/50 lamb and beef is a treat)?

"There are only two things our customers have, time and money—and they don't like spending either one of them, so we better sell them their hamburgers quickly."

—*James McLamore, founder of Burger King*

"You can find your way across this country using burger joints the way a navigator uses stars … We have munched Bridge burgers in the shadow of the Brooklyn Bridge and Cable burgers hard by the Golden Gate, Dixie burgers in the sunny South and Yankee Doodle burgers in the North … We had a Capitol burger—guess where? And so help us, in the inner courtyard of the Pentagon, a Penta burger."

—*Charles Kuralt, award-winning journalist*

WISE MEN SAY

WRAP A GIFT

In many ways the gift wrap is the most important part of gift giving. It creates the first and lasting impression, and beautiful gift wrap can make an inexpensive present look amazing, because it shows that care and effort has gone into the presentation and, by implication, the choice of gift. Always use the best quality paper you can afford.

- ❧ Remember to remove the price tag.

- ❧ If the gift has an irregular shape, find a rectangular box to put it in, then wrap the box.

- ❧ Getting the amount of paper right is the key to neat wrapping;

too much paper will result in bulky seams and end flaps. Place the wrapping paper pattern-side-down on a table or other flat surface and wrap it around the (square or rectangular) gift, cutting enough paper so that there are two inches of overlap on top, then trim the other edge so that you don't have too much overlap at the ends.

•• Place the gift in the center of the gift wrap and fold over an inch of paper along the longest edge. This will create a thicker seam and make the paper look more expensive. Bring the two longest edges together on top of the gift, and tape the folded seam over the other edge, pulling the paper tight so that it fits snugly around the gift. Use a tape dispenser, or cut off lots of two-inch strips in advance and place them on the edge of the table, leaving your hands free for maintaining the correct paper tension.

"It is said that gifts persuade even the gods."

—*Euripides, 5th-century BC dramatist*

"Every gift from a friend is a wish for your happiness."

—*Richard Bach, author*

WISE MEN SAY

•• The gift is now sitting in a tunnel of paper. Turn the gift so that one of the open edges is facing you. Press two vertical sides inward and smooth them against the edge of the box, and tape. Then press the two horizontal sides inward and smooth them against the edges of the box, and tape. Crease at the edges of the box to define them.

Rest the box on its closed end and repeat the previous step on the remaining open end. Push the box downward as you crease the edges, to get a tight fit.

- Turn the box over so that the seamless side is on the bottom. Wrap a piece of ribbon lengthwise around the box, twist the ribbon at the seam, then wrap the ribbon around the box widthwise. The seam will now be completely covered. Tie a double knot where the ribbon meets on top of the box, then cut the ribbon, leaving about six inches to spare.

- Slide one corner of a card or gift tag underneath the ribbon and secure it with a small piece of tape.

- Make each end of the ribbon curl decoratively by trapping them in between your thumb and the blade of a pair of scissors, then pulling the ribbon gently through.

SPEED-READ

Whether you read novels for pleasure or business reports because your job demands it, there are ways to increase your reading speed without sacrificing comprehension. In today's knowledge-hungry age, being able to integrate information quickly and efficiently is a priceless talent.

DEFINE YOUR READING OBJECTIVES

You must know what you want to gain from reading a document as well as the type of document you are reading. For example, if you were reading a novel for pleasure, at the most basic level you would want to understand the story line; if you were reading it in greater depth (e.g., for study purposes), you would be looking for themes, stylistic features, narrative strategies, character analysis, etc. If you were reading a business report to pick out salient points for a presentation, you would search for information to back up and support your own analysis, and you might even need to retain certain facts in fine detail. So, know what you are reading, and why you are reading it.

READ BLOCKS OF WORDS

Children learn to read first by recognizing the letters of the alphabet, then individual words, and increase their fluency until they can read a phrase or full sentence. Speed-reading takes this one step further by focusing on reading blocks of words, rather than a string of individual words.

AVOID REGRESSING

In the West we read by moving our eyes from right to left across the page. Many people, however, frequently move back to a word or group of words to check meaning. This is called regressing. It is very common, but unfortunately it has been shown not only to reduce speed but also comprehension, and it is much more tiring for the eyes, which in turn leads to poorer concentration.

> "I took a speed-reading course and read War and Peace in twenty minutes. It involves Russia."
>
> —*Woody Allen, actor and director*
>
> "I am not a speed reader. I am a speed understander."
>
> —*Isaac Asimov, prolific author and editor*

WISE MEN SAY

Speed up your reading by consciously reducing the number of times that your eyes regress. Aim to keep your eyes moving smoothly from left to right, using your moving finger as a guide, if necessary, to force you to keep up the pace, rather than making (often) unnecessary checking regressions.

HOLD THE TEXT FARTHER AWAY

Sometimes the simple act of holding the text farther away can dramatically increase your eye span and the size of the word blocks that your eye and brain can process.

READ KEY WORDS

Look for the key words in a sentence; these are the verbs, nouns, and adjectives. Don't get hung up on little words like "the" and "and." Your brain will fill in the other words, as long as you focus on the important words that hold the sense and the action.

STOP THE INTERNAL DIALOGUE

You may not actually mouth the words while you are reading, but many people read silently to themselves, saying and/or hearing the words in their head. This is called sub-vocalization and is a major factor in slower reading. Think the words instead of speaking or hearing them.

SUSTAIN CONCENTRATION

Read only when you are feeling fresh and totally focused. If you sense that you are losing concentration, take a five-minute break, move your body around, then return to the task with your full attention.

SPOT A LIAR

The following techniques to spot a liar are often used by police and security experts. Human beings are very expressive animals, and they give away lots of nonverbal cues that reveal their emotions, level of anxiety, intentions, and even which part of their brain they are accessing. Even the best liars are betrayed by their bodies. To spot a liar you just need to recognize the signs.

EYE CONTACT

Poor liars find it difficult to maintain good eye contact, and they will look away frequently, and may even look toward a door or window as if subconsciously trying to escape. They may also overcompensate, however, by trying to hold your stare, and in that case it will feel forced and unnatural. Nevertheless, this is further complicated by the fact that in many Eastern and African cultures it is considered disrespectful to maintain eye contact.

"No man has a good enough memory to be a successful liar."

—*Abraham Lincoln, former U.S. president*

"No one is such a liar as the indignant man."

—*Friedrich Nietzsche, philosopher and author*

WISE MEN SAY

EYE POSITION

Watch for a change in eye direction. When people are accessing memories their eyes tend to go up and to the left (to the right, from your point of view). When people are inventing things (i.e., lying) they tend to look down and to the right.

CHANGE IN PHYSICALITY

The liar's form of physical expression often changes, either becoming more agitated or more limited. Some liars become immobile in the face and body in a subconscious attempt to conceal their thoughts. At the other end of the physical spectrum, excessive fidgeting or playing with the face (liars often cover their mouths, touch their chins or throat, or rub their eyes) may be indicative of lying.

Look for a "closed" body position: arms or legs crossed defensively across the body, or the body turned away from the interrogator. Hand and arm movements often become limited as the subject tries to take up less space (literally, to disappear). Hands may be hidden in pockets or behind the back.

SPEECH PATTERNS

Liars often speak quickly; it's as if they want to get the conversation over with posthaste, so that the focus will pass elsewhere—the verbal equivalent of handling a hot potato! Also, watch out for excessive detail. Liars tend to add details to their original story, whereas truth-tellers stick with their version of events. The pitch of the voice may also rise with the anxiety level of the liar.

Liars often repeat the expressions of their interrogators; for example, answering "Did you borrow my car?" with "No, I did not borrow your car."

Liars often become confrontational in an attempt to prevent further inquiries. Aggressive responses such as "Are you calling me a liar?" are a dead giveaway, as are hyperbolic assurances such as "Never in a million years."

HOW TO TRIP UP A LIAR

Try to position yourself so that you are higher than they are: if they are sitting down, stand up. Make sure your own body language is open and responsive and that there are no obstacles between you. Go silent and allow the other person to fill the awkward pause with further justification and lies. Change the subject; an innocent person will feel the need to pull the subject back again and further vindicate themselves, whereas a liar will happily go along with the new topic, relieved that maybe they have convinced you of their innocence.

BREAK UP WITH A WOMAN TACTFULLY

Breaking up is painful and takes courage and diplomacy. Unless you have both lost that loving feeling, chances are that your girlfriend will feel hurt, confused, betrayed, and even angry when you drop your bombshell. You can't change those feelings, but if you follow this advice you will have a better chance of a smooth parting that is firm but respectful.

MAKE UP YOUR MIND

Think very carefully about whether you really want to break up before you tell your partner. It can rarely be a decision you make together. Eliminate as many of your doubts as possible beforehand, so that you won't be persuaded to change your mind. However, being firm in your resolve doesn't mean you should be cold and distant.

NO PAIN, NO GAIN

Break-ups are usually painful. Accept this, and recognize that a little bit of pain now will lead to better times in the future. Staying in a relationship that makes you unhappy will only lead to more suffering.

DON'T BE A COWARD

Always break up with someone face to face. Only cowards break up by phone, email, fax, or text. Don't fool yourself that you are sparing her feelings by breaking up long-distance, or not returning her calls. You owe it to her to explain your reasons in person rather than expect her to "get the hint."

MEETING UP

Arrange to meet in a public place, so that it is harder for either of you to become visibly emotional and cause a scene. If you break up at your place, then you will have to get her to leave, whereas if you are somewhere neutral and public you can decide when to go. If you are living together, then one of you will have to move out, but it is still best to broach the subject in public where you have a better chance of discussing matters rationally.

BE HONEST, BUT NOT TOO HONEST

Don't blame her for the split, but don't blame yourself either. Try to explain honestly why you want to end the relationship but don't go into too much detail. If you want to play the field, for example, keep that to yourself. Just say that you don't feel ready to commit to a long-term relationship.

IT'S OVER

Be clear that the relationship is over, rather than make vague noises about "needing some space" or "a cool-off period" which will make her think that you may get back together.

Don't let her persuade you to give the relationship one more chance, and don't confuse things with that tempting break-up romp. She may start to cry or yell, and if you still care for her as a person, it will be hard to see her upset, but that doesn't mean you should cave in. Your long-term happiness is at stake here. After several weeks apart you may find that you miss each other and want to get back together, but it is vital that you make a clean split now and follow through.

"Love does not begin and end the way we seem to think it does. Love is a battle, love is a war; love is a growing up."

—*James A. Baldwin, writer and Civil Rights activist*

"There is one thing I would break up over, and that is if she caught me with another woman. I won't stand for that."

—*Steve Martin, comedien and actor*

WISE MEN SAY

HELP A HANGOVER

As the old maxim goes "An ounce of prevention is worth a pound of cure," but if you are planning a heavy drinking session, there are several steps you should take to reduce the after-effects the next morning, and they begin before you even go out.

WHEN THE NIGHT IS STILL YOUNG

1. Never drink on an empty stomach. In some countries (such as France) alcohol is sensibly viewed mainly as an accompaniment to a meal, and drinking for its own sake is discouraged. When your stomach is empty, the alcohol enters the bloodstream more quickly.

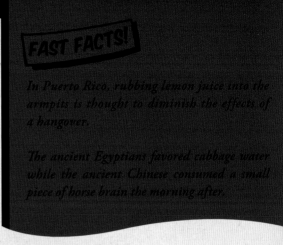

2. Don't mix your drinks. Alcoholic drinks contain chemicals called congeners to improve their taste and color. Mixing different drinks creates a chemical cocktail that really punishes your liver.

3. Drink light-colored, flat drinks. Dark drinks contain more chemicals than light ones. So port and red wine will give you a worse hangover than equivalent units of gin or white wine. Red wine contains tyramine, which contributes to a hangover all by itself, and there's lots of it in cheap red wine. The bubbles in fizzy drinks like Champagne also speed up the absorption of alcohol into the bloodstream.

4. Alternate your drinks. If you follow each alcoholic drink with a soft one, you'll drink less alcohol and increase your hydration.

5. Spread out your drinking over an evening. If you consume less than one unit per hour your body will be able to break it down faster than you are pouring it in.

AFTER THE PARTY

1. Drink three pints of water before bed and don't take any painkillers, such as headache tablets. Instead, eat something with a low glycemic index that releases energy slowly throughout the night. Avoid sugary food. Protein, fat and vegetables can be found in a kebab, so it's not such a bad option at the end of a drink-fueled evening. Alcohol inhibits your kidneys' ability to absorb water, so you pee it out rather than using it in your body's cells. It also strips your body of electrolytes (body salts), vitamins, and blood sugar, and makes you sleep badly (being passed out for the night doesn't count as quality shut-eye).

2. Take a multi-vitamin before bed, as the water-soluble ones like B and C will be peed out during the evening. Vitamin A is fat-soluble, but it will also be depleted by alcohol consumption.

THE MORNING AFTER

1. Take a hot shower to open up constricted blood vessels and to relax your muscles, both of which may ease a neck-tension headache.

2. Avoid caffeinated drinks such as coffee and colas. Drink lots of water at room temperature (too hot or cold and it will stress your system further). Avoid alcohol: hair of the dog will only prolong the hangover.

3. Avoid milk and dairy products, which are hard to digest and will irritate your stomach.

4. Keep drinking lots of water throughout the next day. One of the causes of a hangover headache is brain shrinkage: your body needs water so it steals it from anywhere it can, and this includes your brain. When your brain shrinks, pain-sensitive filaments that attach it to your skull become stretched and cause a throbbing head sensation.

5. A lumberjack breakfast has plenty of hangover benefits: protein is a good source of amino acids and eggs contain cysteine, used to make glutathione, which is depleted by drinking alcohol.

6. Get some fresh air: open the window, or go outside. Oxygen improves the metabolic rate and increases the speed at which the alcohol is broken down.

TRACE YOUR FAMILY TREE

While finding out about your ancestors is fascinating and can be highly addictive, it also requires a formidable degree of orderliness. If you think you'll enjoy keeping exacting records and meticulously filing all of your important discoveries for easy cross-referencing, that's great. If not, you'd better develop some organizational skills fast if you want to investigate your genealogy successfully.

SET GOALS

Before you begin your research, set your goals, and decide what you want to achieve and why, otherwise you could spend months gathering insufficient information, and have to go back to square one to fill in the gaps. Don't expect to trace your family tree all at once. Break each area down into manageable sizes, otherwise you will quickly become overwhelmed and discouraged. If you get stuck, move on to something else and find other angles from which to approach the information you require.

KEEP CAREFUL RECORDS

Don't just write down information that you discover, record your sources (e.g. book title, microfilm number, newspaper, website, date, page number, author, publisher, etc). Document all your tracks, and photocopy all your printed source materials, otherwise you will waste time searching for scraps of information you already have, but can't locate. Keep a contact log which records all the people you meet or correspond with by phone, mail or email.

BE CREATIVE

Use the library, visit a parish church; in small towns, stop by the school, town hall or local paper. Plan ahead so that when you visit you can find the answers to several questions at once.

ORAL HISTORY

Interview all of your living relatives and ask them to show you photographs of their ancestors. Ask them about their childhood experiences, education, work and family life, as all these things help to build a wider picture that will inform your genealogical research. Be aware that oral accounts are also susceptible to human error and inaccuracies of memory.

ASCENDANT CHART

The most user-friendly way of recording your family tree is to start with the present and build a chart of ascendants. Before you start, find out if anyone else in your family has started a family tree so you don't waste time duplicating their work. The diagram begins with you and then leads backwards in time. Turn a sheet of paper horizontally, and write your name and date of birth halfway down in the left hand margin. Write your father's name above and to the right of your name, and your mother's below and to the right of your name. Include their dates and places of birth (and death if applicable) and marriage. Continue to work left to right across the page adding two sets of grandparents and great-grandparents and so on in the same way. You could also use genealogical software (many different versions are available online), but make sure you back up your files regularly. Either way you will need a paper-filing system to keep copies of birth and marriage certificates and other relevant documents.

CONFUSED? YOU WILL BE

Genealogy is rarely straightforward, but the challenge is part of the fun. Be prepared to come across inconsistencies, face obstacles and be forced to make judgment calls. Human error inevitably creeps into written records, with names and dates copied incorrectly or illegibly, so the more sources you can gather relating to each piece of information, the better. Your patience and dogged persistence will pay off. For the truly ambitious, a paleography course can help you read ancient text!

"The past is never dead. It's not even past."

—William Faulkner, Nobel Prize-winning novelist

"I don't have to look up my family tree, because I know that I'm the sap."

—Fred Allen, comedien, radio host

WISE MEN SAY

BOWL A STRIKE

This hugely popular game has been around for ages; the general idea of rolling a ball and knocking things over may date back 5,000 years to ancient Egypt. If you have never bowled, however, you need to know a few basics. One thing you must remember is not to cross the thick black line at the beginning of the lane. This is the foul line. Crossing it scores "F"—zero points.

FAST AND DRY LANES

The lane is made out of boards of wood or a synthetic material and is sixty feet long, but that's not all. The lane is "dressed" with mineral oil, so that some sections are faster than others, which enables a bowler to get "hook" (curve). There is usually more oil in the center than on the outside. If a lane has lots of dressing it is "fast," and if it has little it is called a "dry" lane. Use a towel between turns to wipe oil from the ball. The dryer the ball, the better it will curve.

BALL WEIGHT

Bowling balls range from between 6 lbs up to 16 lbs in weight. As a rule of thumb you should choose the heaviest ball you can manage, but you should be able to hold it with a straight arm in front of you for five seconds without tiring. The heavier the ball the smaller is the chance of it being deflected off course when it strikes the pins. When you've found the correct weight, buy your own ball for bowling consistency.

HOLDING THE BALL

There are usually three holes in a bowling ball. Place your ring and middle finger in the "back" two holes and your thumb in the other. Some bowlers like to place almost their entire digits into the holes, while others use only their fingertips up to the first joint. The fingertip hold is harder to master but is supposed to allow a bowler to achieve greater lift and hook on the ball.

SCORING

Each knocked over pin is worth one point. A strike is when you knock over all 10 pins with the first ball. The score is marked as a 10 plus the total of the next two balls. A spare is when you clear the pins in two balls; the score is 10 plus the next roll. A perfect game is 300 points which requires 12 strikes.

AIM

Look at the pins as you make your approach. Aim to hit the pins at the pocket, which is the space between the head pin and the one next to it on the left (for a left-handed bowler) or right (for a right-handed bowler). If you hit the head pin you will probably end up with a split instead of a strike.

APPROACH

Most bowlers take four steps before releasing the ball. The first step is called the "push away" and comes off the same foot as your bowling hand, while you push the ball forward. During the second step (the "prozone"), you allow the ball to swing backwards, helping you to generate momentum. During the third step (the "pivot") the ball continues to swing backwards until it reaches its apex, and the fourth step is the "slide"—the ball moves forward and is released before the end of the sliding step. Bend your knees as you release the ball.

Some bowlers use a five-step approach, by adding a little step at the beginning which helps them to flow into the next four steps.

HOOK AND SPIN

If you are physically strong, throw your shoulders open on the back-swing to make it very high, with your wrist cranked and elbow bent. Delay the swing so that you have to use a lot of muscle to deliver the ball. Bowlers who use this modern technique are called crankers. It requires power and strength, but the leverage that is generated by this style of shot allows a lot of hook and makes the ball spin very fast.